KENO WINNING WAYS

Figure 1. A $25,000.00 winning Keno ticket played by the author and his "business" partner and a draw showing the winning numbers.

KENO WINNING WAYS

Wayne McClure

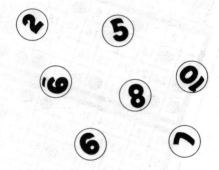

Press

630 South 11th Street
Box 4115
Las Vegas, Nevada 89106

ISBN   0 - 89650 - 779 - 3

CONTENTS

ILLUSTRATIONS

KENO WINNING WAYS

INTRODUCTION

Keno is a fascinating game of chance which pays the highest odds of all the gambling games in Nevada. A wager of less than one dollar can win as much as $25,000 and wins of this amount are paid out quite frequently. The game is now played in most every casino throughout Nevada, continuously, twenty-four hours a day.

It's enjoyed by millions of men and women of all walks of life. These players are mostly vacationers who come to Nevada from all parts of the world. Many are from neighboring states with the greatest number from California.

During the short history of Keno in Nevada (it was first played legally in 1936) it has grown to be one of the most popular of all games of chance. Hundreds of millions of dollars are wagered on Keno annually and its popularity continues to grow.

A Keno game is a drawing of numbers; twenty numbers are selected at random from a total of eighty and the object of the game is to guess which numbers, or at least some of the numbers, that will be drawn.

Keno tickets printed with eighty numbered squares are used to record the players' bets. These tickets are furnished by the house, also crayons for marking them, and to play the game you simply pick up one of these tickets and mark a spot on the numbers you wish to play, in the margin of the ticket write the price of your wager and the amount of spots that are marked.

The amount of spots to mark (one to 15 for straight tickets) as well as which numbers to mark them on is the

1

player's choice. Present this ticket with the amount of the wager to a Keno writer who will make a copy of your ticket. This duplicate copy is returned to the player and is a receipt for the wager.

After the wager is made there is nothing else to do except wait for the results of the drawing and then determine if the ticket is a winner and if so, how much it has won.

Tickets are also furnished at the bars and in the restaurants so that patrons can conveniently play while enjoying refreshments or eating. Keno runners will pick up your tickets from these areas, play them for you and return the receipted copies.

When all tickets are written, which might require five to ten minutes or more, the drawing of the game begins. The game is drawn by mixing eighty ping-pong balls, numbered from one to eighty, and at random drawing out twenty of them. The numbers on these twenty balls become the winning numbers for that game and are recorded in lights on flashboards located throughout the casino and most of the bars and dining areas. Also, after each drawing, special blank tickets with the winning numbers punched out are available. These punched tickets are known as "draws" because they show the results of the drawing for each game. These draws are used as a convenient method for checking the winning numbers with the spots marked on a ticket. By placing the draw over a ticket the winning spots may be viewed through the holes in the draw. Also, one draw from each drawing is always filed as a permanent record. When the drawing of the game is completed, which takes about two minutes, winning tickets are paid off and new tickets are written on the next game. A ticket that has been played on a previous game can be replayed from the receipt copy without marking a new ticket.

A wager can be made on any amount of spots from one to fifteen and as many tickets as desired may be played on each drawing.

More than fifteen spots on one ticket can also be played, which will be explained later.

The amount of money that a ticket can win depends on the amount of the wager and the number of spots being played. Figure 2 is a schedule of ticket costs and payoffs, showing the winning catches for each ticket and the amount each catch wins for the listed ticket price. The catch on a ticket is the amount of spots (the numbers that are marked) which appear in the twenty winning numbers.

The lowest ticket prices shown in figure 2 indicate the minimum wager for most casinos. However, unlike most other games which have a usual betting limit of $200 to $1000 per wager, there is no maximum betting limit on a Keno ticket. Therefore the wager on a Keno ticket can be any amount in even multiples of the minimum rate, and the amount of the win is in proportion. The limit on a Keno game establishes a limit of liability for losses on each drawing, which is $25,000 in most Nevada casinos. A limit is necessary on all forms of gambling and this is the most practical method of establishing a limit on this type of wager.

Keno, in its basic form, is quite simple. It's easy to play. The cost is small and the amounts that can be won are very large. All of this, and especially the attraction of the big payoffs, make it one of the most popular games of chance in Nevada.

There are many advanced methods of play that have been developed over the years and some of these are very complex. Newcomers to the game are often amazed at its operation and seem confused when they see some of the tickets that are played. And terms like "way tickets," "kings," "combination tickets" and "pawns" add to the confusion and make the whole game seem as though it's shrouded in mystery.

These mysteries are explained in the following pages.

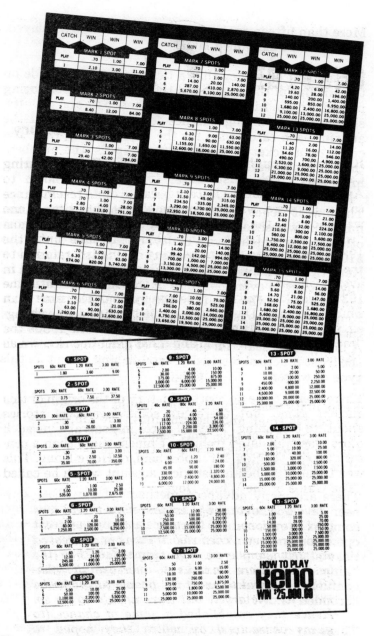

Figure 2. Schedule of ticket costs and payoffs used in 1978 & 1979.
Figure 3. Ticket pay rate used in the late 1960s and early 1970s.

4

CHAPTER

History

Keno was brought to America by the Chinese during California's gold rush days. It was then known to Americans as Chinese lottery because of its resemblance to our lotteries, which were popular at that time. Keno was known to the Chinese as Pak Kop Piu, which means "white pigeon ticket," and from that time until the 1930s the Chinese, when speaking in English, referred to the game as "pigeon lottery." This game was played in every Chinese settlement in America and, until the 1930s, was known to Caucasians by no other name than Chinese lottery. During the 1930s the name was changed, first to Race Horse Keno, and then in the 1950s the "race horse" was dropped and it has since been known as "Keno."

Origin

There seems to be no written history of the origin of this ancient game, but there are some legendary stories about its beginning. They all agree in general. One such story was translated from the Chinese more than a century ago by the Rev. Mr. Lobscheid, of Hong Kong. This was thought to be an historical account which he called "The Game of the White Dove."

> *"This game is an old establishment, and was first introduced by Cheung leung of the great Han Dynasty. When the city was hard-pressed and provisions were beginning to fail, they (the besieged) were anxious to increase the contributions and to exort the people to subscribe more for the army, but were unable to do so. Hence they established a game of chance (to guess characters) by which they hoped to tempt the people to hazard their property. In order to fix a method of losing or gaining at*

hazard, they chose 120 characters for the whole game and eighty characters for one subdivision.

"If the people lost one (whole) subdivision they lost three li; if they gained one division they were rewarded with ten taels.

"These regulations being once established, who would not sacrifice a little in order to gain much? The two games in the morning and evening were attended by men and women who tried their luck by guessing. They had only operated the game for about ten days when they had accumulated more than 1000 pieces of silver; and after a few more decades their wealth was boundless.

"The money thus gained was considered a contribution to the army for the reduction of the empire."

This account establishes the time of the game's origin as between 205 and 187 B.C. It does not, however, state precisely how the game was first played, and so is typical of the early accounts of most games. It seems that the early-day writers assumed that the reader was entirely familiar with the details of how the game was played.

Later on, the game was changed and practiced as a profession.

With the new plan, eighty characters from the Thousand Character Classic were chosen for the whole game, ten characters forming one division, which the people were permitted to purchase for any amount they pleased. Each player, in order to win, must guess five or more of the winning characters. A wager of three cash guessing five characters would win five li; when six characters they win five candarens; when seven characters they win five mace; when eight characters they win two taels and five mace; when nine characters they win five taels; and when ten characters they win ten taels.

6

The amount of characters "guessed" was later referred to as being "caught." This came about from a strange way of expressing the likeliness of a win. *The Chinese envisioned eighty mountains with twenty loose monkeys, and calculated how many monkeys might be caught by ten soldiers searching one mountain each.* The amount of spots marked on a ticket which appear in the twenty winning numbers has since been referred to as the *"catch."*

From the time of the new plan through the present day the game has remained basically the same, the only changes being the addition of new ticket wagers, an occasional change in the payoffs (winning odds) and the different methods used in selecting the winning numbers.

Pak Kop Piu In Canton

John Henry Gray, Archdeacon of Hong Kong, wrote an account of the game as it was played in Canton in 1861:

"Large sums are daily lost by men, women and children of all classes, in a game called Ta-pak-up-pu, or 'strike the white dove.' A company is formed, consisting of fifty partners having equal shares. One is selected to act as an overseer, and, for reasons which will presently appear, he is made to live in strict retirement. A sheet of paper on which eighty Chinese characters, respectively signifying heaven, earth, sun, moon, stars, etc., is given to him. With this sheet he enters a private apartment and remains there without communicating with any one for several hours, during which he marks twenty of the characters with a vermilion pencil. The sheet is then deposited in a box, which is at once carefully locked. Thousands of sheets of paper containing eighty similar characters are then sold to the public. The purchasers mark ten of the eighty, and take their papers next morning to the gaming establishment to have them compared with that marked by the overseer. Before they give them up, they make copies of them which they retain. When all the papers have been received, the box which contains the overseer's paper, and which stands conspicuous on a table, is unlocked. The gambler's papers are then compared with the overseer's paper. If a gambler has marked only four of the characters selected by the overseer, he receives nothing. If he has marked five of them he receives seven cash; if six, seventy cash; if eight, seven dollars; and if ten, fifteen dollars. A person wishing to gamble can buy as many as three hundred copies of the gambling sheet, but he must mark them all alike."

This account fails to state the amounts won for marking seven or nine of the winning characters, or the amount the tickets sold for. It does, however, establish another method by which the game was once played.

Pak Kop In Philadelphia

An account of this game as it was played in Philadelphia in 1880 was written by Stewart Culin, secretary of the museum of Archeology and Paleontology of the University of Pennsylvania:

"A very popular gambling game among the Chinese is a kind of lottery known as Pak Kop Piu, which signifies 'white pigeon ticket.' In China, where lotteries are illegal, they are frequently carried on among the hills near the cities, and it is said that pigeons are used to convey the tickets and winning numbers between the offices and their patrons; whence the name applied first to the tickets and from them to the lottery itself.

"In America the offices of the Pak Kop Piu are always located in an upper room, suggesting the survival of the use of the loft, from which the messengers were formerly dispatched. But no such precaution is necessary; the mails carry the tickets, and runners daily traverse the cities from laundry to laundry, soliciting custom. Pak Kop Piu is always carried on by a company, which assumes an auspicious name, in the same manner as the store companies, and has an office, where the drawings are conducted, usually in a room over a shop. (It is customary for the store companies to act as bankers of the lotteries and guarantee payment of the prizes.) This office consists of a small compartment, with a strong railing in front, extending midway from the floor to the ceiling, which permits a full view of the interior. Wooden shutters are frequently used to close this railed space during the day.

"The drawings take place every night. Between 9 and 10 o'clock the pak kop piu sin shang, as the manager of the lottery is entitled, lets down the

8

wooden shutters, locks himself in his cage, and is prepared to sell tickets for the drawing that takes place that evening.

"The tickets for the pak kop piu are imported already printed from China in large quantities, and invariably consist of pieces of unsized paper about five inches square, upon which have been printed from a wooden block in black, blue or green ink, the first eighty characters of the Ts'-in-tsz'man, or Thousand Character Classic. *(The tickets used in the United States are now largely made in San Francisco, and are invariably printed in green or blue ink.)* This book, which contains precisely one thousand characters, no two of which are alike, is so well known in China that its characters are frequently used instead of the corresponding numerals from one to one thousand. They serve the purpose of numbers on the tickets.

"Twenty of the eighty numbers are drawn every night. The company sells each player ten or more numbers, and pays prizes to those who purchase a certain number of characters drawn. A player prepares his tickets by dotting the characters he selects with black ink, and this ticket is handed to the manager, with the money wagered. He has a number of blank tickets, bound in the form of a book, on one of which he marks the corresponding characters, and writes the player's name and the amount. Ten numbers are sold on the basis of one dollar and this is the usual form of the wagers. When the office is open, the runners and agents, and such customers as have not entrusted them with their commissions, present their marked tickets, with the money, and see that their bets are duly recorded.

"About an hour after letting down the shutters the drawing takes place. Eighty pieces of white paper have been provided, upon which have been written or printed the eighty characters of the tickets, one on each, a box of hand stamps for the purpose, forming part of the equipment of most lotteries. The manager carefully rolls the eighty pieces of paper into as many pellets, so that they cannot be distinguished, one from one another, and places them in a large tin pan. He mixes them thoroughly, and then, one at a time, counts twenty of the pellets into a white china bowl, distinguished by a white paper label marked 'one.' He then counts twenty more into another bowl labeled 'two,' and, in turn, places the remainder, in the same way, into two other bowls marked, 'three' and 'four.'

"One of the players, who is paid a small gratuity, is now asked to select one of the bowls, and the one he designates is declared to contain the winning numbers. These the manager carefully unrolls, one at a time, at once pasting them on a board in the back part of his office.

"The spectators watch every movement, and cheating is difficult. It is almost impossible for the company to direct it against the players, but the manager sometimes contrives to defraud the company by arranging that certain numbers shall win, about which he has informed the players with whom he is in collusion, in advance of the drawing.

"Those who purchase ten numbers lose their stakes unless they happen to have bought at least five of the winning numbers. Those who guess five or more of the winning numbers receive the following sums for each dollar they wager:

For 5 winning numbers	$ 2.00
For 6 winning numbers	20.00
For 7 winning numbers	200.00
For 8 winning numbers	1,000.00
For 9 winning numbers	1,500.00
For 10 winning numbers	3,000.00

The companies, however, always deduct five per cent from these amounts, and when the ticket has been sold through an agent, fifteen per cent, ten per cent of which is paid to the agent. Proportional sums are paid when the amount wagered is less than one dollar.

"Most of the companies sell more than ten numbers, from ten up to twenty, at a proportional advance in price as the player's chances are increased, and the prizes vary from those paid when ten numbers are sold. The price which should be charged for more than ten numbers, with the prizes to be paid, and the methods of calculating the company's chances, and what its profits should be, are contained in a book known as **pak kop piu t'o**, of which several editions are current among the gamblers in American cities. One in general use, entitled **'Shang ts'oi tsit king,'** or *'A quick way to get rich,'* may be purchased in the Chinese shops.

"The manager of the lottery must have special knowledge of the business. He, and his assistant who prepares the papers for the drawings, are dignified with the title of **Sin shang**, literally 'first born,' which is equivalent to Mr., and is about the only title of respect used among the Chinese laborers in America.

"The principal manager is paid from forty to sixty dollars, and his assistant from thirty to fifty dollars per month, for their two hours' service at night, in addition to which they usually have some remunerative employment during the day. They may have a share in the lotteries, but are not permitted to purchase tickets.

"When the winning numbers are declared, messengers at once carry tickets on which they are marked with red ink, to the Chinese stores and restaurants, where they are prominently displayed. Many of the stores act as agents for the lotteries, and charge purchasers fifteen per cent commission. The runners also charge fifteen per cent advance, so that their customers pay one dollar and fifteen cents for ten numbers, of which they turn in one dollar to the manager. Anyone can buy tickets at the office without paying a commission, but most of the tickets are sold through agents, as they can sell them for amounts as low as ten cents, while the offices usually will not receive less than one dollar from others. Besides, they insure their customers against mistakes in marking their tickets, the companies being very ready to decline to pay prizes on account of such errors. The winner must be paid on the following day, and failure to pay results in the destruction of the business, but this is of very infrequent occurrence. The lotteries are often compelled to suspend, however, through their capital being exhausted by repeated losses. The cash capital required is not large. In 1886 there were four pak kop piu companies in Philadelphia, known as the **Kwong T'ai,** 'Extensive Increase,' **T'in Wo,** Heavenly Harmony,' **Fuk T'ai,** 'Fortunate Increase,' and **Ch'iu Ts'un,** 'Encourging Fountain.' In New York there were five, and numerous companies exist in the Chinese colonies of Boston, Chicago and the larger American cities.

"Another form of this game, known as Shan Piu or 'Mountain Lottery,' is occasionally opened by Chinese gamblers in American cities. It is played with the same tickets and in the same manner as pak kop piu, and differs from it in the entire receipts from the sale of tickets, less the company's commission, being divided among the players who guess the largest number of characters."

The Shan Piu version of this game might be considered a true lottery because every drawing resulted in the awarding of a designated prize.

This is a very good account of how the game was played when introduced into America. Only minor changes have been made since.

Sometimes when drawing a game the Chinese used no containers, just mixing the wads on a table with a short stick and separating them into four equal piles. Various methods were used to determine which pile would be chosen as the winning numbers. Usually one of the players was asked to select one of the piles. On some Caucasian games the twenty winning numbers were selected by drawing five random numbers from each of four bowls, each bowl containing twenty random numbers.

It has been said that this game was often played in China without the use of tickets:

If the group participation was very small, they would write the characters being wagered on in the palm of the hand. These characters were not revealed to the party operating the game, and their fists were kept closed while the winning characters were being selected so as to prevent the players from changing the written characters in their hands. When the winning characters were declared anyone who had a winner must immediately open his fist and prove it. This method of playing the game would seem satisfactory only with a very small group.

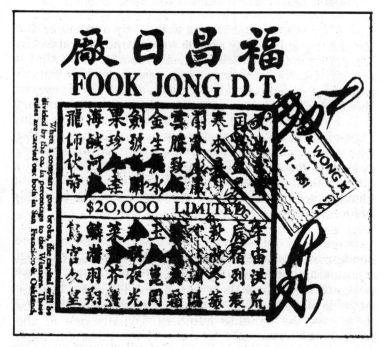

Figure 4. A Chinese lottery ticket that was actually played on a game in San Francisco.

Shown in figure 4 is an old Chinese lottery ticket from San Francisco. Through the center of these tickets was usually printed a message of advertisement.

13

This one shows the pay out limit.

The wording on some of the early tickets read: *"Imprinted according to the original copy."* The characters in the body of this ticket represent the eighty numbers. These characters are the first eighty of an ancient poem known as the "Thousand Character Classic."

An Ancient Poem

There are various stories about the origin of this poem. Some scholars generally agree that it was written between 507 and 521 A.D. by Chou Hsing-szu. Others believe it was written about 255 A.D. by someone unknown. Legendary stories differ also.

One story relates that it was written by a minister during the Liang Dynasty and he was liberally rewarded by the emperor for his achievement. Another says that it was written by a prisoner as an assignment for punishment for a crime. Another reference states that these one thousand characters were written during the 6th century A.D. by the celebrated penman Wang Hi-che on as many slips of paper. The Emperor Liang Wu Ti then directed Chow Hing-sze to arrange them in rhymed sentences to convey a meaning. This task was accomplished in a single night, but such was the mental effort that the compiler's hair and beard were turned completely white before morning.

It is really an old poem and was used in China as the second primer for teaching reading and writing to children. By putting one thousand characters into a more or less coherent rhymed form, learning was presumably made easier and more interesting. It is something of a very great achievement in that no character is repeated. This poem was so well known in China that its one thousand characters, arranged in order, was often used as a fanciful way of notation or counting from one to a thousand. These characters on the Chinese lottery tickets are used only to represent numbers.

14

Translation

The Chinese language is so different in origin and structure from Western languages that it is usually impossible to make a meaningful literal translation. This is especially the case with material such as this, which is written in the old Classical style — extremely condensed, with no punctuation and often cryptic (even to Chinese) in precise meaning. If ten Western scholars sat down to make a translation, you always would have ten different results, agreeing in a general sense but varying in detail of the choice of words and sentence construction.

The poem is read from the upper right column down to the bottom and continues from the top of each column to the left.

The generally accepted trend of thought is translated here, numbered from the start of each sentence as it's located on the ticket:

10. sky earth mysteries yellow
50. universe infinite vast space
9. sun moon full declining
49. stars lunar arrange widely
8. cold come heat go
48. autumn harvest winter storage
7. intercalary surplus complete year
47. musical instrument harmonize nature
6. cloud ascend cause rain
46. dew frozen create frost
5. gold make beautiful water
45. jade from high mountain
4. sword label high gate
44. pearl called night shine
3. fruit precious plum crabapple
43. vegetables important mustard ginger
2. sea salty river saltless
42. scales submerge feathers soar
1. dragon teacher fire emperor
41. bird official human sovereign

15

From this condensed translation it can be realized that some of the meaning must have been lost, and the construction of these sentences could be completed in many different ways. A construction of these sentences as made by Dr. Morrison and published by Stewart Culin follows:

10. Heaven and earth black and yellow;
50. The canopy of the universe, wide and waste;
9. The sun and moon, full and waning;
49. The stars and constellation arranged and set out.
8. The cold comes and the heat goes
48. The autumn is for ingathering and the winter for hoarding up
7. The intercalary superfluities complete the year
47. And the notes of the gamut adjust the superior principle of nature.
6. When the clouds ascend on high, they occasion rain;
46. When the dews concrete they become hoar frost.
5. Gold is produced at the "graceful water;"
45. Gems come from the "Kuan lun hill."
4. Of swords, the most distinguished is the "Great Chamber;"
44. Of pearls, the most celebrated is the "Night Splendor;"
3. Of fruits, the most precious are the damson and the plum;
43. And of vegetables, the most important are the mustard plant and ginger.
2. The sea water is saltish, and the river water fresh.
42. The scaly tribes plunge deep, but the feathered soar high.
1. The dragon (designated) a teacher (in the time of) "the Fire Emperor,"
41. While birds were the mark of offices under the "Human Sovereign."

While the use of these characters on the tickets only represent numbers, some Chinese people select the characters to be marked for their word meaning. rather than for the number they represent. The words selected often have some significent meaning to them. It may be pronounced the same as their name, or may link to some recent event or a thought that has just occurred to them, or it may allude to a recent dream. They have many ways of selecting the characters they wish to play. Many Chinese people in America today know this poem and mark the numbers that correspond to their selected characters. Some Nevada casino tickets are printed with these characters superimposed over the Arabic numerals.

CHAPTER

Chinese Lottery in the West

The Chinese started emigrating to America in 1849, and from that time until 1951 most every Chinese Settlement in America had as many lottery games in operation as their community would support. Chinese people are generally fond of gambling, and during the 1930s many gambling houses operated in each of many Chinatowns in the larger American cities. Most of this gambling however was forms other than Chinese lottery.

San Francisco's Chinatown supported, perhaps, the greatest number of lottery games of any American city. There were seventeen games operating there during the 1930s, each under a different company name. It's been said that the main offices for these games were located in the City of Oakland, which is situated just across the Bay from San Francisco.

These games held two drawings each day, which was also the general custom throughout America. The drawings were held at about 2 p.m. and at about 8 or 9 p.m. and to distinguish between them they were referred to as the day game and the night game. Some of these games would take in more than $3,000 in wagers on a single drawing.

These games had agents which were located throughout Chinatown. Local merchants; restaurant operators, grocers, etcetra, sold tickets in conjunction with their regular business, acting as agents for the lottery companies: Taking wagers which were registered with the main office prior to each drawing. Agents received a commission of fifteen percent of the wagers they handled, and the payment of all wins from their action was made through them. The player never knew where the drawing was held or who was backing the game.

A ticket could be played on a specified company's game or it could be played simultaneously on as many different games as the agent represented; a separate wager on each. Tickets could also be played on as many future drawings as the player desired. The use of runners, to solicit customers, was also common on all of these games.

The 10 spot was, by far, the most popular of all tickets. It carried a usual minimum wager of ten cents, while some of the games accepted this ticket for a five cent wager. The second most popular ticket was the 9 spot, followed by the high-low, and then by the 11 spot and 12 spot tickets. The 8 spot, 13 spot, 14 spot and 15 spot tickets were also played but, because these minimum wagers were so high (similar to those listed on page 86), they were played only on rare occasions. These tickets were not serially numbered, but were certified with a hand stamp showing the date and game (day game or night game) on which they were played, as shown in the illustration in figure 4.

The payout limit on these games varied usually from about $2,000 up to $20,000, while some of the games operated with a $30,000 limit. One game operated for about nine months with a $35,000 limit. (The Chinese operated a game in Vancouver, British Columbia during the 1920s with a limit of $50,000.)

The limits set on these San Francisco games applied to each agent individually, and for that reason some players would play the same ticket numbers with several agents. Then in the event of a limit win they would be able to collect the limit from each agent with whom they had wagered. That is if the company was not bankrupt.

After the turn of the century many small towns in the West were well known for their Chinese lotteries. Several games operated in towns along the Sacramento River up to Marysville and through the Sacramento Delta Area. Also the towns of Virginia City, Reno and Elko in Nevada, and the towns of Butte and Great Falls in Montana, just to name a few, had lottery games for many years. Most of these games had a liability limit of from one to two thousand dollars per drawing.

In 1951 there were eleven games operating in San Francisco when a new Federal Tax Law became effective requiring all such operations to register with the Internal Revenue Service by obtaining a wagering tax stamp, which cost $50, and then pay a ten percent tax on all wagers. These games were subject to this wagering tax only because not all of the participants were present at the drawing. This type of gambling was illegal in California, and the purchase of a wagering tax stamp would be self-incriminating, so this act closed most of the Chinese lotteries games.

CHAPTER

Caucasians Learn The Game

A few Caucasians worked on some of these early Chinese games, and after about 1915 there were several Chinese lotteries operating throughout the West by Caucasians. Robert Fitzsimmons learned this game from the Chinese in Montana and operated the lottery games on all the gambling ships that were anchored off the coast of Los Angeles from 1928 to 1939.

These games were operated from behind a caged counter, as was the custom at that time, and the drawings were conducted with four coffee cans and eighty cardboard squares, about three-fourths inch in size, on which the numbers were written. All of the cardboard squares were put into one can for mixing, and then divided, at random, twenty into each can. The game manager then moved the cans about, as a gesture of mixing them, and at random picked up one declaring it to contain the winning numbers. These cardboard squares were quite durable and lasted for many days before it was necessary to replace them. As these squares were removed from the winning can they were laid on the counter and the number was announced. Another writer punched these numbers out of some blank tickets to record the results of each drawing. These blank tickets were dated with a hand stamp and were also numbered to show the corresponding game number. This was necessary as it was the custom in those days to allow a winner seven days to present a winning ticket for payment. These results were also shown on a board which was made up similar to the flashboards of today, except they were not lighted. The numbers were painted on a white surface and each was covered with a hinged flap which was opened, as the game was drawn, to show the winning numbers.

There was a $1,000 payout limit on these games which operated on a twenty-four hour basis with three to ten writers on each of three shifts. Unlike the Chinese games which were customarily drawn twice daily, this is the first known operation which drew games continuously. They averaged about four draws each hour.

About ninety-five percent of the tickets written were 10 spots which could be played for a 15¢ minimum wager. Other tickets played were 35¢ 9 spots and 55¢ 11 spots. No form of a way ticket was accepted on these games.

There may someday be a feature added to this game such as four draws per game where all the numbers are drawn and separated into four groups of twenty each. These draws could be numbered one, two, three and four for each game and a ticket could be played on any numbered draw desired or on all four draws at the same time. This could be operated on the same basis as the single draw of today, as the probabilities would remain the same.

Other Caucasian Games

Pete Naughton also learned this game from the Chinese in Montana; his gambling house in the City of Butte featured a Chinese lottery in 1928. By 1934 there were four such games operating there by Caucasians. One or two Chinese games were also still in operation. Caucasians also operated games in Great Falls, another mining town in Montana, but all gambling there was continually being closed by local police (more so than in Butte); they were able to operate only about six months out of each year. These games, which were mostly referred to as just "lottery," continued in Montana until 1948.

The tickets for the Caucasian games were printed in Arabic numerals, as they are today, and were slightly smaller in size than today's tickets. (The tickets of today measure five and a half inches by five and three-fourths inches.) There were no lines on these tickets separating the numbers, which was also the way all Chinese tickets were printed.

24

Among the Caucasian gambling halls in Butte, Montana were the M&M Bar, Walkers, 30 Club, Board of Trade and the Crown Cigar Store. The latter was owned by Pete Naughton, the stepfather of Joe and Francis Lyden who were pioneers in the Nevada gaming industry. These business establishments were open from about 9 a.m. until 2 a.m. By 1930 the custom of drawing only two games each day had been changed and since that time all Caucasian games have drawn continuous games throughout their business hours.

The earlier games in Butte were constructed in the usual Chinese fashion, a counter enclosed with cage-work extending about half-way to the ceiling. The drawings were conducted on the counter in the usual Chinese fashion, and a board on the back wall was used to paste the winning numbers on for display after each drawing. The winning numbers were also marked on a blank ticket, by marking a spot on each, as a means of recording the results. Later on the games were drawn with balls and the game-result draws were made with a hand operated punch. The draws were dated with a rubber stamp, as were the tickets. It was the custom there to allow a player fourteen days to present a winning ticket for payment.

On the counter, tickets were furnished for the players, also a supply of ink and brushes for marking them. These brushes were typical Chinese writing brushes, the same as used today, about the size of a pencil with a round bristle about one inch in length tapered to a point. The ink supplied for the players' use was regular laundry bluing, which is still used in some clubs. As these tickets were presented for play, duplicate copies of each was made with black ink on tickets that had a number printed in the upper right corner, to correspond with the game number of the next drawing. These duplicate tickets were given to the players as a receipt for their wager. At the time of each drawing the original tickets (the ones presented for play by the players) were picked up from each writer and placed on the desk in one stack. These tickets then comprised the recorded wagers of that drawing, and after they were checked for wins they

25

were bound in the form of a book with a staple through the upper left corner.

If an error was made in duplicating one of these tickets it had no effect on the bet as all winning pays were made according to the tickets submitted for play by the players. The duplicate copies acted merely as a receipt of the wager to identify the party to whom a winning pay would be made. (There was a time when the Chinese did not make duplicate copies of tickets and the players then signed each ticket played for the purpose of identifying the winner.)

In event a mismarked ticket was replayed on another drawing, it would become the wager of record and the bet would be changed accordingly. For many years this had also been the custom on all Chinese games in America.

As these tickets were copied (written) a hand stamp was used to date them which also printed a duplicate serial number (usually four digits) on each. The date was necessary because at that time a winning ticket could be cashed up to fourteen days after the drawing. (It was common then to have tickets played that were not checked for wins until later in the day or until the next day.) The serial number was used to quickly locate the original ticket when the duplicate copy was presented for payment of a win.

It was in about 1928 when the first hand operated numbering stamp was used to serially number the tickets. Joe Lyden was first to use serial numbers and got the idea when he observed a druggist using such a device to print duplicate prescription numbers.

Secret Ink

Before the use of serial numbers the owners of winning tickets had been identified in several ways. In ancient times a player signed his ticket for this purpose, and duplicate tickets were then not made. After duplicate tickets were made the owner of a winning ticket identified himself by presenting the duplicate copy. As a prevention against fictitious duplicate copies, these game operators used a special ink to mark these tickets which only they could identify.

With the use of serial numbers the type of ink used to write the duplicate copy tickets was of no real importance. However, to add mystery to the game, a special ink was used by all the game operators in Montana. The manager would go into a back room alone and mix it, and it was rumored to the players that its secret formula could never be duplicated.

It was usually made from Chinese ink by adding vermilion pigment, some laundry bluing, sometimes a sprinkling of starch and often other ingredients of no particular value, just to make it appear different from other inks.

These secret inks were used until about 1936.

For many centuries the only ticket played was the 10 spot, but by 1934 all amounts of spots from one to 15, except the 5 spot, 6 spot and 7 spot tickets, were being played as standard (straight) tickets. This totaled thirteen different tickets in play, including the high-low. The tickets that were mostly played during the 1930s are shown in figure 15, however the minimum wager on some was a different amount from those shown here and the usual payout limit was then $2,000. The 10 spot was the most popular. It carried a ten cent minimum wager and could be played for any desired amount above the minimum. The average wager per ticket at that time was about twenty-five cents and the average volume of wagers per day was approximately $600. Each game employed about four people, which were always men.

During the 1930s the volume of play on the games had increased to a point that it was desirable to increase the efficiency of operation. Writing tickets was more simple when only 10 spots were played, as it was necessary then to write only the amount of the wager in the margin of each. But with many different tickets in play the amount of spots marked on the ticket was also written in the margin. And on way tickets it was necessary to show how the wagers were applied to each way. During this time the Roman Numeral X was adopted for use instead of the Arabic ten for conditioning the 10 spot ticket, perhaps because it was more easily written. This practice remains the custom on most games today.

The preparing of numbered papers and the wadding of them for each drawing was a very time consuming operation, and was really not a very good method, as it gave the operator a chance to manipulate some of the numbers. For instance, if the operator should write a ticket for a customer with a very large wager on it and wanted to make certain that it did not win, he was able to do so. He would remember the numbers on that certain ticket and while wadding the papers in preparation for the draw he would make those wads different from the others. They would be wadded tighter or looser or with a certain little twist so that they could be distinguished from the others. Then while mixing and separating them into the four bowls these wads would be evenly distributed, so that whichever bowl was selected as the winning numbers this "big ticket" could not catch enough numbers to win.

Other Methods of Drawing

In the early 1930s, to increase efficiency, Warren Nelson made some changes in the method of drawing the games. For his first change, short pieces of surgical rubber tubing was used, and instead of wadding the papers they were rolled and inserted, one into each tube. (Instead of paper, small squares of linen cloth were also used.) Now these tubes were drawn as the wads had been, by mixing and dividing them equally into four containers. When the winning container was selected, the pieces of rubber tubing were removed, one at a time, the paper was unrolled and the number announced. As each number was announced the paper was held out, being turned from side to side for viewing by the players. These same papers were used for each drawing — which saved preparing new ones. This was in about 1931. *(A method*

28

similar to this was used by some Chinese operators in China. Instead of rubber tubing they used bamboo shoots and after the winning numbers were attached to a board for display, the remaining numbers were destroyed by burning.)

Within a week or so the pieces of rubber tubing were replaced with large capsules, about one inch in length, and the drawing procedure remained the same.

Figure 5. An old-fashion Keno goose. This is the type of receptacle used to draw the numbers for the original game of Keno.

(photo courtesy John Brown)

While the capsules were in use an experiment was made in a new method of selecting them. A board with eighty holes, as explained on page 62 was used for only a few days, then back to the four bowls.

Figure 6. A wire cage Keno goose. This type is used on some games today. *(photo courtesy Club Cal Neva)*

While this method of drawing the games was much quicker than with the wads it still required several minutes to complete. And it was about this time that the games had begun to operate on a continuous basis so an even quicker method of drawing was needed. Capsules were used to draw the games for only a very short time, then a keno goose and numbered balls were used.

A Keno goose, illustrated in figure 5, was the device used to draw the numbers on the original Keno game. Originally, Keno was the name of the game which is known today as bingo. (It was not until the 1930s that the term "Keno" was associated with Chinese lottery.) The original Keno game was played then just as bingo is played today, except there was no "free play" on the center square.

To accomplish the draw with the Keno goose the balls were mixed by rotating the goose and were drawn, one at a time, by tipping the neck downward and actuating a trigger mechanism. This trigger mechanism in the neck of the goose allowed only one ball to escape each time it was triggered. (The earlier goose had no trigger mechanism and in its stead the operator used his thumb over the spout.) This method of drawing the game was much faster than with wads or capsules and the players liked it much better.

The old-fashioned goose was used for about one year until the present day type of wire cage, shown in figure 6, was introduced. This was in about 1932 or 1933. The wire cage was much larger than the old goose and the balls being larger and also visible made a much better appearance. Numbered ping-pong balls were used, the same as today, and the wire cage was operated in the same manner as the old goose. As each ball was drawn it was placed in a rack for viewing and the cage was again rotated before drawing the next ball. Another writer punched the draws, by punching a hole through the winning numbers of a blank ticket, as the balls were drawn.

The drawing of a game in this manner required only about one or two minutes. This type of drawing made the operation of the game more efficient and, except for one more experiment in about 1947 or 1948 with punchboards, the winning numbers on all Caucasian games have since been drawn with balls.

CHAPTER 4

Keno In Nevada

Montana is thought of as the proving ground of this game for Caucasians, as it was from there that the game was introduced into Nevada.

Gambling was legal in Nevada until 1910 and was again legalized on March 20, 1931. During the time that it was illegal gambling continued however, just as it did in most other states. In the City of Reno, as in the City of Butte, most forms of gambling, except lotteries, were so openly conducted that it was difficult to visualize it as being illegal. Lotteries being prohibited by the Nevada State Constitution prevented the Chinese lottery games from operation in the open during the time that gambling was illegal and also after other forms of gambling was legalized. Nevertheless, there were Chinese lotteries that operated almost continuously during all of this time. One such game was located near the Southwest corner of Lake and Second Streets in Downtown Reno. This game operated from the 1920s (and perhaps much earlier) until 1956. This establishment was known as the China Club and was operated by Walter Tun from 1935 until his death in 1946, then by his daughter until the business closed in 1956.

Nevada Gambling Is Legalized

The bill which again legalized gambling in Nevada was introduced on Friday the 13th of February 1931, and listed the authorized forms, enumerating them as: Faro, Monte, Roulette, Keno, Fan Tan, 21, Black Jack, Seven and a Half, Big Injun, Klondyke, Craps, Stud Poker, Draw Poker, or any banking game played with cards, dice, or any mechanical device. This bill was signed into law on March 20, 1931, and it did not include Chinese lottery because this game was considered to be a lottery.

This prevented the few existing Chinese lottery games, which were operated by Chinese, from operating legally.

In Elko, Nevada on March 19, 1931 Henry Leong, a Chinese restaurant operator, applied to the City Clerk for a license to operate a Chinese lottery game. *(At that time there was no Gaming Commission and gaming licenses were issued by local government agencies.)* Leong was informed that such a license could not be issued, that the bill to legalize gambling had not yet been signed by the governor, and even when it is signed it does not permit the conducting of a lottery.

It seemed that the main objection to the game was its name and, because of its name, it was considered to be a lottery.(Lotteries were also prohibited by the Montana State Constitution and the objections to the game there were the same as in Nevada.)

So, in Butte, Montana in about 1935, a change was made in the game in an effort to make it more acceptable. This is the time that the game was first called *"Race Horse Keno."* By that time the games had been drawn for some time with a Keno goose and the original game of Keno, which is known today as bingo, was fast becoming known by names such as beano, bingo and tango.

The original game of Keno was an old established gambling game. It was popular in England, on the Mississippi River boats and in the gambling houses throughout America.

Keno is a derivative from the word, "quine," meaning five, and in this original game the first player to get five beans in a row was the winner and announced it by shouting quine or keno. During the 1920s and 1930s (and also today) many social organizations played this game of keno for the purpose of raising funds. They mostly called it beano or bingo, rather than keno, because the word "keno" was then more associated with "hard gambling." These new names made the game more acceptable to the societies of some organizations. (During the latter part of the nineteenth century the word

34

"bingo" was a slang term for brandy, but by this time it was no longer known as such.) This game was then played with seventy-five numbers, as it is today, where it had previously used ninety numbers. (During the mid-1800s in the gambling halls of San Francisco, one hundred numbers were also used.)

A *goose* had always been used to draw the numbers on this keno (bingo) game.

The goose, referred to as such because of its long goose-like neck, contained seventy-five balls about the size of large marbles (about one inch in diameter), which were made of a hard rubbery-like composition (various colors were used), each bearing one number. Each ball had a slight indentation on which the number appeared.

So, to give the Chinese lottery game a "face lifting" and because the games were drawn with a Keno goose and also because the original Keno game was getting to be known as tango and bingo (the first bingo parlor Bill Harrah opened in Reno was in 1937 and it was known as a tango parlor) it was natural to rename the lottery game and call it Keno. But because the original Keno game was still remembered it was necessary to differentiate between the two Keno games. The term *"race horse"* made the difference. Warren Nelson selected the names of eighty race horses and these names were printed beneath the numbers, as shown in figure 8A.

This name change in Montana did very little toward further promoting the game as the old-timers there had known it for such a long time as Chinese lottery. After about 1940 the games in Montana were mostly referred to as "lottery."

Race Horse Keno Comes To Nevada

Francis Lyden had worked on his stepfather's Chinese lottery game in Montana for some time, and in 1936 he was working in the Palace Club in Reno when he proposed to the owners, the Petricciani family, that they install a Chinese lottery game, call it Race Horse Keno, and operate it in the same fashion as the games in Montana. The Petricciani family realized the attractive features of this high-odds game of chance and were aware of its success in Montana. An agreement was made whereby Francis made no financial investment but would supervise the operation for a certain percentage in the venture.

Preparations were made and on the second day of May, 1936 the first Race Horse Keno game of Nevada opened for business.

In the bill to legalize gambling, Keno was included as an authorized form, and it might seem that race horse Keno would have been a recognized game. But the game referred to in the senate bill was then known as bingo and the licensing authority considered Race Horse Keno to be a "cover up" for a lottery.

So the first application for a license was denied.

Figure 7A. A view from behind the counter on the first Keno game in the Palace Club (1936). This is the only Caucasian game in Nevada to have cage-work around the counter.
(photo courtesy Palace Club)

To obtain a license John Petricciani and Peter Merialdo called on the governor in Carson City and was able to make a convincing presentation that the game was a

36

"banking game" and was played with a "mechanical device." Race Horse Keno was then recognized and a license was issued.

Figure 7B. The Palace Club's Keno game after it was remodeled in 1939.
(photo courtesy Palace Club)

The tickets used on this game were the same as those used on the Race Horse Keno game in Montana, as shown in figure 8A. During the drawing of each game, as each ball was drawn, the number was announced as a jockey of that number riding the corresponding horse. As time went on some of the games adopted different sayings with the calling of each number, such as number 16: "It's jockey number 16 riding 'main street,' and there they go right down the main drag, it's a helluva race."

Each drawing was then referred to as a *race* rather than as a *game*, and oldtimers today sometimes make reference to a race. Later on some of the games further imitated a horse race by announcing when ten balls had been drawn that *"they are now at the half-way mark"* and when fifteen balls were out, *"they are now in the homestretch."*

All but two or three of the writers who worked on this game during the first summer of operation were from

Montana and included Warren Nelson, Ken Watkins, Jim Brady, Francis Lyden, Clyde Bitner, Johnny Morse, Dick Trinastich, Jack Mullen, Tommy Cavanaugh, Jimmy Crowley, James Kiley, Jim Shay, Joe Hobson and one or two others. At that time these men were among the few Caucasians who were skilled in the operation of this Chinese game, having worked on the games in Montana for several years.

PALACE CLUB
THE HOME OF NEVADA'S KENO GAMES
132
$5,000.00 Limit Each Game
WINNING TICKETS PAYABLE IMMEDIATELY FOLLOWING EACH GAME

1 Nanny D	2 Sanli	3 First Pip	4 Dupee	5 Bert John	6 Don Pedro	7 Old Master	8 Ask Katie	9 Oregon Fir	10 War Tide
11 Rowdy Boy	12 Ancoda	13 Grand Baby	14 Golden Words	15 Roxane	16 Main Street	17 Zembla	18 Double Chin	19 Fly Cop	20 Orbin
21 War Over	22 Fuss Budget	23 Ann T.	24 Voyage	25 Miss Sage	26 Black Velvet	27 Flywood	28 Salona	29 Fair Lever	30 Skid
31 Busy Ike	32 Scotch Tom	33 Stroll Along	34 Bright Bird	35 Wedding Ring	36 On Tap	37 Fiddler	38 Dinner Goat	39 Fog Bound	40 Mixed Party

41 Divert	42 Gold Strike	43 Zip Along	44 No Doubt	45 Moby	46 Lilly May	47 Miss Spray	48 Just Cap	49 Golden Storm	50 Bally Bay
51 Tut Tut	52 Kay C	53 Happy Anne	54 Mintie	55 Town Square	56 Rock Sun	57 Rustic Lady	58 Monel	59 Rufle	60 Kay Dugan
61 Zinn	62 Dark Winter	63 Golden San	64 Lady Conrad	65 Suiter	66 Sun B	67 Tom Proctor	68 Dark Amber	69 Eva B	70 Daudet
71 Black Tom	72 Come Along	73 Big Boy	74 War Stripes	75 Parity B	76 Arch-Wood	77 Flash	78 Shot Gun	79 Red Fox	80 Bright Lady

Figure 8A. The first Race Horse Keno ticket. Designed by Warren Nelson and used on the Palace Club's game.

For the game a counter was built in the usual fashion of that period with cagework extending half-way to the ceiling. And the first electrically lighted game-result flashboard was built and installed before the opening of the game.

Some of the necessary equipment was brought from Montana, which included an old-fashioned Keno goose with which to draw the games. The players of Reno were familiar with Chinese lottery but none had seen this game drawn with a Keno goose. A difference of prob-- abilities was visioned in the two methods of drawing, thinking that by using paper wads and four bowls the twenty winning numbers were selected simultaneously, making the odds something like one in four; when the winning numbers were selected one at a time the odds should change to something like one in eighty, com- plicated with one in seventy-nine, etc. This caused some amount of notoriety which was good advertising for the game.

1 Baggen-baggage	2 Behave Yourself	3 Billionaire	4 Black Toney	5 Blue Larkspur	6 Boiler-maker	7 Brooklyn	8 Brown Jade	9 Bubbling Over	10 Bye Bye Mary
11 Carlaris	12 Ceiling	13 Chance Play	14 Count Morse	15 Dis Donc	16 Display	17 Dominant	18 Epinard	19 Equipoise	20 Exhibit
21 Fair Play	22 Flying Ebony	23 Gallant Fox	24 Grey Streak	25 Happy Bolivar	26 Heel Fly	27 Indian Broom	28 John P. Grier	29 Johnny Dear	30 Lady Higloss
31 Mad Hatter	32 Man O War	33 Matey	34 Miss Mars	35 Misstep	36 Native Daughter	37 Nevada Queen	38 Official	39 Omaha	40 Open Range

41 Phar Lap	42 Pompey	43 Pompoon	44 Prince Pal	45 Privileged	46 Rebellion	47 Reigh Count	48 Rough Party	49 Royal Charm	50 Royal Minstrel
51 Sarada	52 Sea Biscuit	53 Sir Barton	54 Sir Gallahad	55 Sir Satin	56 Special Agent	57 Speed	58 Sting	59 Sun Beau	60 Sweep
61 Table Stakes	62 Tap Time	63 Teddy	64 The Fighter	65 The Porter	66 Tiempo	67 Top Flight	68 Trans-mute	69 Tree Tune	70 Twenty Grand
71 Upset	72 Virnock	73 Well Heeled	74 Whisking	75 Wise Counseller	76 Wise Duke	77 Working Girl	78 Xandra	79 Zzy	80 Zev

Figure 8B. The second Race Horse Keno ticket. It was designed and used by the Bank Club of Reno.

The games were drawn with the old-fashion Keno goose during the first two weeks of operation, then the wire hand cage and ping-pong balls were used thereafter. The hand cage was still referred to as a goose.

The game opened with a $2,000 limit, as this had been the limit in Montana, and the whole operation of the game was fashioned around the customs these men had previously acquired.

Soon after the Palace Club's game opened, the China Club changed the name of its game from lottery to Keno and began to operate legally. However, they continued for some time to draw only two games each day and there was never any competition with the other clubs. This establishment later came to be known as New Star Keno.

The next game to open in Reno was on April 7, 1937 in the Bank Club.

Clinton Dalton, who had worked for several years on the game in the M & M Bar in Butte, Montana, supervised the operation of this game. And the original crew, like that of the Palace Club game, was also mostly from Montana. This crew consisted of about twelve men and included Johnny Yersin, Bruce Dalton, Joe Hobson, Martin Din, Hank Freudenstein, Jack Dorlan, Benny Peck, Ronald Gibson, Mike Ausich and Windy Sholls.

A new set of horses' names was compiled for these tickets, as shown in figure 8B. This game also opened with a $2,000 limit and operated on a twenty-four hour basis in the same fashion as that of the Palace Club.

In about 1938 the limit on these two games was changed to $5,000 and this remained the highest limit on any Nevada game for the next sixteen years. This seemed to be an extremely high limit because the game was still new to Nevada, even though some of the games in San Francisco were operating with a much higher limit.

On September 26, 1940 Harolds Club opened its Race Horse Keno game. (Games had been opened there prior to this date by two or three parties who were unsuccessful.)

Figure 8C. The third Race Horse Keno ticket. It was designed by Harolds Club of Reno.

This game opened with a $5,000 limit and another set of race horse names was compiled and used on these tickets, as shown in figure 8C. Warren DeMaris supervised operations. He had previously worked on the lottery game in the Board of Trade in Butte, Montana and on games in Portland, Oregon and so was well-qualified. Most of his crew was also made up of men from Montana, the source for experienced writers.

The next game to open was in 1944 in the Reno Casino. This game was opened by Chet Gonce who compiled another set of horses' names for these tickets. Some of the names selected were those of actual race horses but most were fictitious.

The Nevada Club started a Race Horse Keno game when they opened for business in 1946 and, in keeping with the trend, another set of race horse names was compiled for their tickets.

Another set of horses' names was compiled for the second game in Harolds Club which operated for about a year on the second floor during the latter 1940s.

Not many of the other games which opened in the area after this time used race horse names; most of those which did used one of these sets.

At this time other clubs began to open throughout the state and the number of Keno games increased. In 1948 there were seven games in Reno and all, except the New Star Keno, were operating with a $5,000 limit; about this same number of games were scattered throughout the balance of the state. Only those games that used race horse names on their tickets were known as Race Horse Keno, the others were referred to as just "Keno."

$25,000 Limit

On August 2, 1954 the Frontier Club in Reno opened a game with a $10,000 limit and within a week all the games in town had raised their limits accordingly. There were then nine games operating in Reno. This game was opened by R. H. "Pick" Hobson and Jim Brady who recall a $10,000 win that occurred on about the third day of operation. It was a 10 spot ticket and all the spots were caught.

At about this time the Horseshoe Club in Las Vegas raised its limit to $25,000. The Frontier Club in Reno then raised their limit accordingly and within a year most of the games in Reno were operating at this higher limit. By 1959 almost every game in the state was operating with a $25,000 limit, where it remains today.

42

(Since April, 1963 the sum of $25,000 has been fixed by the Gaming Commission as the maximum limit on any one Keno game.)

Just Keno

By 1948 some of the clubs had discontinued the practice of calling out the horses' names as the games were being drawn; however, for a time the numbers were called as a jockey of that number only. *By this time the original game of Keno was known in Nevada as bingo and it was no longer necessary to use the term "race horse" to distinguish one game from the other.* This game was generally known as Race Horse Keno until 1951 when some of the clubs began omitting the horses' names from their tickets. The term "race horse" was then less frequently used, and by about 1960 the horses' names had vanished from all tickets. The game has since been known just as Keno.

Occasionally, on games operated by oldtimers, when it's nearing time to draw a game it's referred to as post time.

As the balls are drawn the numbers are announced and, for clarity, it is customary to state the word "number" before those numbers along the top, one through 10, and before those along the right side of the ticket, 10 down through 80, and also before number 12. This prevents any misunderstanding when certain numbers are drawn in sequence, such as when number 40 is followed by number 6.

New Ticket Rates

The pay rates of tickets have changed many times since 1945. In 1947 a "Keno War" existed for two weeks in Reno when all the games continually increased the winning pays until the margin of profit was insufficient to pay expenses. Then all the games went back to the standard rates shown in figure 9, which were used on most all games until 1954.

43

KENO RATE SCHEDULE
$5,000.00 Limit Each Game

9 Keno Rate

Kenos	35c Ticket
4	.15
5	1.80
6	17.80
7	110.70
8	373.50
9	738.00

10 Keno Rate

Kenos	50c Ticket
5	1.00
6	9.00
7	90.00
8	450.00
9	900.00
10	1,800.00

11 Keno Rate

Kenos	55c Ticket
5	.60
6	5.10
7	42.30
8	207.00
9	585.00
10	1,080.00
11	1,980.00

8 Keno Rate

Kenos	2.60 Ticket	6.40 Ticket
3	.25	.65
4	3.95	9.95
5	37.15	92.90
6	258.70	646.75
7	1,138.65	2,846.70
8	3,126.60	5,000.00

13 Keno Rate

Kenos	2.85 Ticket
5	1.10
6	8.55
7	53.10
8	241.40
9	774.00
10	1,866.40
11	3,591.00
12	5,000.00
13	5,000.00

14 Keno Rate

Kenos	5.00 Ticket
5	1.25
6	9.25
7	53.50
8	234.55
9	756.00
10	1,900.00
11	3,912.00
12	5,000.00

15 Keno Rate

Kenos	7.50 Ticket
5	1.25
6	9.00
7	48.85
8	207.00
9	665.75
10	1.706.40
11	3,412.80
12	5,000.00

Figure 9. Schedule of pay rates used during the 1940s & early 1950s.

High-Low Ticket, 12 Kenos

3 groups of 4 — 35-cent rate pays

5 kenos	2–2–1	pays	.20
	3–1–1		.25
	3–2		.30
	4–1		.35
6 kenos	2–2–2		1.50
	3–2–1		1.80
	3–3		2.40
	4–1–1		2.40
	4–2		2.65
7 kenos	3–2–2		11.35
	3–3–1		14.25
	4–2–1		17.15
	4–3		23.00
8 kenos	3–3–2		56.50
	4–2–2		67.70
	4–3–1		78.85
	4–4		110.30
9 kenos	3–3–3		194.40
	4–3–2		198.00
	4–4–1		205.20
10 kenos	4–3–3		432.00
	4–4–2		450.00
11 kenos	4–4–3		756.00
12 kenos	4–4–4		1,296.00

Figure 9 (continued).

45

While the price war was on, the Nevada Club of Reno introduced a new type of ticket wager known as insurance. This wager could be made on any ticket containing four or more spots and was entirely separate from the regular ticket bet. The insurance wager won only if none of the numbers marked on the ticket were drawn, and winning pays were made according to the schedule shown below:

RATES OF PAY FOR INSURANCE WAGERS

Number of Spots on Ticket	For Each $1.00 Wagered Insurance Pays
4	$ 2.00
5	3.00
6	4.00
7	6.00
8	9.00
9	12.00
10	17.00
11	24.00
12	34.00
13	48.00
14	70.00
15	101.00

Insurance Pay Rates

Insurance wagers could be made in any amount, from ten cents up, and winning pays were made in proportion. To indicate an insurance wager a rubber stamp was used in the margin of these tickets that printed the word "insurance," beneath which was written the amount of the bet. The Nevada Club in Reno and the Nevada Lodge at Lake Tahoe are the only clubs to ever write this insurance. Few players today have ever heard of this insurance, even though it was in effect until May, 1967.

For a time, free insurance, to the amount of the ticket wager, was offered on tickets played on specified games.

46

These games were announced about once every two or three hours and the free insurance was for the purpose of goodwill and advertising. It was common for players to play more tickets on these games than on the regular games because of the increased chances of winning. Players playing one or two tickets on each of the regular games would often play a dozen or so on the insurance-free games. Once a player who had twenty-eight hundred 5 spot tickets marked in preparation for play was waiting for one of these games to be announced when Curtis Harwood, the game manager, informed him that the purpose of such games was only for goodwill and his bet on so many tickets would not be accepted. *The odds on such a wager favors the player by 41 percent*, and the amount of the expected loss for so many tickets was much more than could be considered as goodwill. The free insurance was later discontinued.

In about 1952 the Nevada Club also introduced the High-Low 9 spot ticket. The win rate for this ticket is shown in figure 10. It was marked with 9 spots which were divided into 3 groups, each containing 3 spots, in a manner like the High-Low ticket shown in figure 26. The probabilities of this ticket were computed and the pay rate designed by a professor of mathematics at the University of Nevada who also computed the odds for the insurance wager. This High-Low 9 was never a very popular ticket but was adopted by all of the clubs and remained in play until 1967.

Specials

In 1955 a new pay rate was introduced for the 8 spot ticket and soon afterward for the 9 spot ticket. These rates were referred to as "specials," to distinguish them from the others and the minimum wager on the specials was set at an amount different from the wager on the regular ticket — 55¢ for the specials and 50¢ for the regulars.

With the payout limit increased, these rates were designed to pay larger wins for the greater catches and lesser amounts for the smaller catches. These new rates had a great appeal to the players mostly because of the large wins on the two greater catches. This, and the term "special" seemed to create a difference atmosphere about the whole game.

SPECIAL TICKET RATES

$1.10 – 8 Spot Ticket		$1.10 – 9 Spot Ticket	
Catch	Win	Catch	Win
5	$ 10.00	5	$ 4.00
6	90.00	6	54.00
7	2,200.00	7	350.00
8	25,000.00	8	6,000.00
		9	22,000.00

First special ticket pay rates ever designed.

The smaller catches on these specials paid less than on the regular tickets, but most players were willing to sacrifice there for a chance at the "big money." Not all of the clubs adopted these specials immediately.

Some waited for several years.

And some of the clubs that did adopt them maintained a minimum wager of $2.20 until after 1960. By then most clubs were writing them for a minimum wager of 55¢.

These new rates and the term "special" played a large part in promoting the game. Where the 10 spot had been the favorite ticket most players were now playing the special 8 spot, which remains the most popular of all tickets today. Within three years the game had more than doubled in volume and its popularity has continually increased since.

At about this time new pay rates for a 50¢ wager were designed for all tickets, except the High-Low 9, and these are shown in figure 10 along with the other popular tickets played during the latter 1950s.

$1.00 ONE SPOT RATE	2 SPOT RATE, $.50 up	3 SPOT RATE, $.50 up
Catch one spot, win $3.20	Catch 2 spots, win 13 for 1	Catch 2 spots, win money back Catch 3 spots, win 47 for 1

4 SPOT RATE, $.50 up	5 SPOT RATE 50-Cent Ticket		6 SPOT RATE 50-Cent Ticket	
Catch 2 spots, win money back Catch 3 spots, win 5 for 1 Catch 4 spots, win 118 for 1	Catch	Win	Catch	Win
	3	$ 1.50	3	$ .50
	4	13.00	4	2.80
	5	166.00	5	55.00
			6	620.00

7 SPOT RATE

50-Cent Ticket		50-Cent Ticket	
Catch	Win	Catch	Win
0	$ .50	0	$ 1.00
1	.15	1	—0—
2	.15	2	—0—
3	.20	3	—0—
4	1.00	4	1.00
5	8.00	5	7.00
6	88.00	6	150.00
7	750.00	7	1,600.00

8 SPOT RATE

50-Cent Ticket		55-Cent Ticket	
Catch	Win	Catch	Win
4	$ .50	5	$ 5.00
5	7.50	6	45.00
6	55.00	7	1,100.00
7	447.50	8	12,500.00
8	2,250.00		

8 SPOT RATE

$2.60 Ticket		$6.40 Ticket		$12.80 Ticket	
Catch	Win	Catch	Win	Catch	Win
3	$ .25	3	$ .65	3	$ 1.30
4	3.95	4	9.95	4	19.90
5	37.15	5	92.90	5	185.80
6	258.70	6	646.75	6	1,293.50
7	2,000.00	7	5,000.00	7	10,000.00
8	7,500.00	8	18,700.00	8	25,000.00

9 SPOT RATE

35-Cent Ticket		50-Cent Ticket	
Catch	Win	Catch	Win
4	$ .15	4	$ .20
5	1.80	5	2.55
6	17.80	6	25.40
7	110.70	7	158.10
8	1,000.00	8	1,428.55
9	2,250.00	9	3,214.20

9 SPOT RATE

45-Cent Ticket		55-Cent Ticket	
Catch	Win	Catch	Win
5	$ 1.50	5	$ 2.00
6	20.00	6	27.00
7	165.00	7	175.00
8	2,500.00	8	3,000.00
9	10,500.00	9	11,000.00

10 SPOT RATE / 11 SPOT RATE / 12 SPOT RATE

10 SPOT RATE		11 SPOT RATE 50-Cent Ticket		55-Cent Ticket		12 SPOT RATE 50-Cent Ticket	
Catch	Win	Catch	Win	Catch	Win	Catch	Win
5	2 for 1	5	$ .50	5	$ .60	5	$ .30
6	18 for 1	6	5.00	6	5.10	6	2.60
7	180 for 1	7	38.00	7	42.30	7	18.70
8	1,300 for 1	8	240.00	8	267.00	8	106.50
9	2,600 for 1	9	800.00	9	845.00	9	374.00
10	10,000 for 1	10	1,636.40	10	1,800.00	10	912.80
		11	5,000.00	11	5,500.00	11	1,916.60
						12	5,000.00

Figure 10. Pay rates used during the latter 1950s and early 1960s.

13 SPOT RATE

50-Cent Ticket		95-Cent Ticket		$2.85 Ticket	
Catch	Win	Catch	Win	Catch	Win
5	—0—	5	$ .35	5	$ 1.10
6	—0—	6	2.85	6	8.55
7	$ 9.00	7	17.70	7	53.10
8	53.00	8	100.10	8	300.30
9	460.00	9	360.10	9	1,080.30
10	2,200.00	10	950.30	10	2,851.00
11	4,240.00	11	2,035.00	11	6,105.00
12	6,000.00	12	4,110.00	12	12,330.00
13	8,000.00	13	9,540.00	13	25,000.00

14 SPOT RATE

50-Cent Ticket		$1.25 Ticket		$5.00 Ticket	
Catch	Win	Catch	Win	Catch	Win
5	—0—	5	$ .30	5	$ 1.25
6	—0—	6	2.30	6	9.25
7	$ 5.00	7	13.40	7	53.50
8	28.50	8	70.65	8	282.65
9	197.00	9	253.25	9	1,013.05
10	700.00	10	694.00	10	2,775.90
11	4,000.00	11	1,552.40	11	6,209.50
12	9,000.00	12	3,060.00	12	12,240.00
13	18,500.00	13	5,900.00	13	23,600.00
14	25,000.00	14	13,000.00	14	25,000.00

15 SPOT TICKET

50-Cent Ticket		$1.50 Ticket		$7.50 Ticket	
Catch	Win	Catch	Win	Catch	Win
5	—0—	5	$ .25	5	$ 1.25
6	—0—	6	1.80	6	9.00
7	$ 3.90	7	9.80	7	48.85
8	14.00	8	48.85	8	244.20
9	82.00	9	172.35	9	861.70
10	315.00	10	480.00	10	2,400.00
11	1,300.00	11	1,107.45	11	5,537.30
12	6,000.00	12	2,225.00	12	11,125.00
13	14,000.00	13	4,130.00	13	20,650.00
14	25,000.00	14	7,700.00	14	25,000.00
15	25,000.00	15	16,000.00	15	25,000.00

Figure 10 (continued).

In the early 1960s special rates for other tickets began appearing, and it was customary in most clubs to write a small letter "S" in the conditioning margin of these tickets to designate that they were played at the special rate. When a club introduced a new ticket rate, other clubs would either adopt it or design one of their own or both. This resulted in most of the tickets being played with several different pay rates. By 1966 these rates were so numerous (all of the tickets shown in figures 10

	HIGH-LOW TICKET, 12 SPOTS	
	3 GROUPS OF 4	
	35-Cent Ticket	50-Cent Ticket
Catch	Win	Win
2–2–1	$ .20	$ .30
3–1–1	.25	.35
3–2–0	.30	.40
4–1–0	.35	.50
2–2–2	1.50	2.15
3–2–1	1.80	2.55
3–3–0	2.40	3.40
4–1–1	2.40	3.40
4–2–0	2.65	3.80
3–2–2	11.35	16.20
3–3–1	14.25	20.35
4–2–1	17.15	24.50
4–3–0	23.00	32.85
3–3–2	76.50	109.30
4–2–2	87.70	125.30
4–3–1	98.85	141.20
4–4–0	132.30	189.00
3–3–3	194.40	277.70
4–3–2	198.00	282.85
4–4–1	205.20	293.15
4–3–3	432.00	617.15
4–4–2	450.00	642.85
4–4–3	756.00	1,080.00
4–4–4	1,296.00	1,851.45

Figure 10 (continued).

HIGH-LOW 9			
9 SPOTS, 3 GROUPS OF 3			
60-Cent Ticket			
Catch	Win	Catch	Win
2--1—1	$ .60	3—2—1	10.00
2—2—0	1.00	2—2—2	20.00
3—1—0	1.35	3—3—0	133.35
		3--2—2	166.65
2—2—1	2.00	3—3—1	266.65
3--1—1	3.35		
3—2—0	6.65	3—3- 2	1,666.65
		3—3—3	3,333.35

Figure 10 (continued)

and 11) that an effort was made to standardize the rates and use only one for each ticket.

New rates were then computed for all tickets, except the High-Low 12 and the High-Low 9 spots which were omitted, and were adopted by most clubs in Northern Nevada in May 1967. These rates are shown in figure 3. At about this same time the clubs in Southern Nevada adopted similar rates.

Carryovers

The practice of writing carryover tickets was in effect in 1910; no one seems to know just when it began. This was the term used when a ticket was played for more than one game and paid for in advance. Until 1962 any ticket could be played for as many games in advance as the player desired. The games for which the ticket remained in play were noted on the original ticket and also on the duplicate copy by showing the first and last game numbers. This saved having to go back to the counter to replay the ticket on each game and, for convenience, was practiced by many players. Some who traveled through Reno on regular trips would often stop and play such a ticket *(sometimes for so many games that it would take a few days to draw them all)* and would stop on their

3 SPOT RATE

Catch	55-Cent Ticket	70-Cent Ticket
3	$ 30.50	$ 38.00

4 SPOT RATE

Catch	55-Cent Ticket	55-Cent Ticket	55-Cent Ticket	60-Cent Ticket	60-Cent Ticket	70-Cent Ticket
3	$ 2.50	$ 3.00	$ -0-	$ 3.50	$ -0-	$ 3.20
4	102.00	100.00	137.50	100.00	150.00	130.00

5 SPOT RATE

Catch	55-Cent Ticket	55-Cent Ticket	60-Cent Ticket	65-Cent Ticket	70-Cent Ticket
3	$ .35	$ 1.50	$ .50	$ 1.50	$ .45
4	3.10	13.00	5.50	14.00	4.00
5	550.00	225.00	555.00	300.00	700.00

Catch	70-Cent Ticket	70-Cent Ticket	75-Cent Ticket	75-Cent Ticket	75-Cent Ticket
3	$ .50	$ .50	$ .75	$ .75	$ -0-
4	4.00	3.70	9.00	9.75	-0-
5	700.00	700.00	600.00	600.00	871.75

6 SPOT RATE

Catch	55-Cent Ticket	55-Cent Ticket	55-Cent Ticket	60-Cent Ticket	65-Cent Ticket	75-Cent Ticket
3	$ -0-	$ .35	$ .50	$ .35	$ .40	$ .75
4	5.00	2.80	2.80	3.10	3.00	3.75
5	55.00	50.00	62.50	61.10	65.00	66.00
6	1,000.00	1,100.00	740.00	1,125.00	1,200.00	1,200.00

7 SPOT RATE

Catch	55-Cent Ticket	60-Cent Ticket	65-Cent Ticket	70-Cent Ticket	75-Cent Ticket	$1.25 Ticket
0	$ -0-	$ -0-	$ .65			
4	1.50	.50	2.00	2.00	2.10	2.00
5	10.00	10.00	10.00	14.00	15.00	18.00
6	150.00	265.00	200.00	200.00	210.00	500.00
7	6,000.00	6,250.00	2,500.00	7,000.00	7,200.00	12,500.00

8 SPOT RATE

Catch	35-Cent Ticket	55-Cent Ticket	55-Cent Ticket	60-Cent Ticket	65-Cent Ticket	65-Cent Ticket
0				$ -0-	$ .65	$ -0-
4	$ .50	$ -0-	$ -0-	-0-	-0-	.70
5	2.00	5.00	5.00	5.25	6.00	5.00
6	25.00	45.00	45.00	50.00	86.00	50.00
7	515.00	1,000.00	1,100.00	1,200.00	500.00	1,125.00
8	5,000.00	14,000.00	12,500.00	13,750.00	3,500.00	12,500.00

Figure 11. Special ticket rates used from 1964 to 1967.

	9 SPOT RATE			
Catch	40-Cent Ticket	45-Cent Ticket	55-Cent Ticket	55-Cent Ticket
5	$ 1.30	$ 1.50	$ 2.00	$ 1.65
6	18.00	20.00	27.00	25.00
7	145.00	165.00	175.00	175.00
8	2,200.00	2,500.00	3,000.00	3,300.00
9	9,500.00	10,500.00	11,000.00	16,500.00

Catch	60-Cent Ticket	65-Cent Ticket	$1.10 Ticket	$1.25 Ticket
0	$ —0—	$ .65	$ —0—	$ —0—
5	2.25	2.00	3.30	5.00
6	29.00	25.00	50.00	60.00
7	190.00	259.00	350.00	400.00
8	3,250.00	1,800.00	6,600.00	5,000.00
9	12,500.00	5,000.00	25,000.00	10,000.00

	10 SPOT RATE				11 SPOT RATE		
Catch	55-Cent Ticket	55-Cent Ticket	65-Cent Ticket	Catch	65-Cent Ticket	70-Cent Ticket	
0	$ —0—	$ —0—	$ 1.00	0	$ 1.00	$ —0—	
5	.50	—0—	—0—	5	—0—	.70	
6	6.00	10.00	10.00	6	5.00	6.00	
7	90.00	100.00	100.00	7	40.00	47.00	
8	1,100.00	900.00	1,000.00	8	372.00	311.00	
9	5,000.00	4,000.00	2,000.00	9	1,000.00	1,111.00	
10	25,000.00	16,000.00	10,000.00	10	2,000.00	11,111.00	
				11	12,500.00	25,000.00	

	12 SPOT RATE		13 SPOT RATE		14 SPOT RATE		15 SPOT RATE	
Catch	60-Cent Ticket	65-Cent Ticket	Catch	65-Cent Ticket	Catch	65-Cent Ticket	Catch	65-Cent Ticket
0	$ 2.00	$ 1.00	0	$ 1.00	0	$ 1.00	0	$ 1.00
6	3.00	2.00	7	10.00	7	5.00	7	4.00
7	22.00	20.00	8	63.00	8	35.00	8	15.00
8	128.00	176.00	9	500.00	9	200.00	9	100.00
9	450.00	500.00	10	2,500.00	10	1,480.00	10	400.00
10	1,000.00	1,100.00	11	4,500.00	11	5,000.00	11	2,400.00
11	2,000.00	2,200.00	12	10,000.00	12	10,000.00	12	10,000.00
12	10,000.00	15,000.00	13	20,000.00	13	20,000.00	13	20,000.00
					14	25,000.00	14	25,000.00
							15	25,000.00

Figure 11 (continued).

return trip to check the results. They were allowed seven days after the last game was drawn to claim a win, and as such a ticket was considered to be one wager, a win produced from any draw could not be collected until after the last game was drawn.

This practice of writing carryovers continued until August of 1962 when the Internal Revenue Service applied a tax ruling to this type of wager. This ruling required the payment of a wagering tax of ten percent which applied to all lotteries. Their definition of a lottery, for the purpose of this ruling, was any game of chance where the wagering participant was not present. This was not intended as a description of a lottery, but to define the games of chance that were subjected to this wagering tax. This tax applied not only to the carryover tickets but to all ticket wagers; there not being a ten percent net profit in the game forced all casinos to discontinue this practice.

This caused the rule that is printed on the tickets today which states that all winning tickets must be cashed in (presented for payment) before the start of the next game (time of the next drawing).

A Strange Game

Prior to 1946 the game of Race Horse Keno was, by far, the least known of any of the casino games of chance. It was common to have visitors who had frequented the casinos for some time who had never played this game and had no idea how it was played. There were occasions when it was common for several hours to pass without a single wager being made. Customers would often inquire how it was played, make one wager and leave, never realizing the object of the game.

Once in Harolds Club a gentleman asked how to play the game and when it was explained to him, he played a 15¢ 10 spot ticket. When the duplicate copy was given to him, he asked how long a time it was good for. Warren DeMaris, the game manager, replied that it was good for seven days, thinking that he meant the length of time that the ticket could be cashed in for a win. This man had never seen a game like this. He sat at a vacant 21 table and watched all the draws for the next two hours, then brought the ticket back to the Keno counter (none of the draws had produced a win) saying that he was on his way to New York and didn't have time to wait for all the drawings — they could have his ticket! It was only then that they realized his false impression of the wager. They thanked him and never told him that the wager applied to only one drawing.

Once a lady thought she had won $3,600 when a game was drawn and she had caught one spot on her 15¢ 10 spot ticket. A sign on the wall read "you can win 3600 for 1" and she thought this meant for catching one spot. These were the winning odds at that time, for catching all the spots on a 10 spot ticket, and it was the customary method of expressing the 10 spot pay rate, as all the pays were in even odds for one. She was very disappointed when the game was further explained to her.

Some tickets are played today by players who bring them back to the counter after the drawing and ask how many spots they must catch to produce a win. In 1964 a lady disposed of a 55¢ 8 spot ticket in a waste basket because she had caught only 7 spots and thought that all 8 spots must be caught to win. When she arrived home and related the story to her friends, they informed her that she had thrown away a ticket worth $1,100; it's well to know the rules of any game!

A winning ticket worth $1,920 was once left at a Keno counter even after being presented for payment. This was in 1962 and microfilm equipment had just been installed on this game for photographing the tickets prior to each drawing. When the winner, a middle-aged man, presented the ticket for payment he was told that it would take a few minutes to develop the film before payment could be made. By the time the film was developed and payment approved the man had disappeared and was never seen again. Apparently, the man thought the film being developed was a photograph of himself and that he must have been wanted by some police agency. Or, perhaps, he was in a place where he wasn't supposed to be!

Many winning tickets of various amounts are never cashed. It's quite common today, especially on the larger games, to have one or two winning tickets each year of a thousand dollars or more that are never presented for payment. One game in 1959 had a $25,000 winning ticket that never showed up.

CHAPTER 5

More Keno Games

Keno's popularity began to increase considerably in 1946, and during the next several years many casinos throughout the state were opening Race Horse Keno games. This increase in the volume of wagering brought about certain changes in the operation of the game. Prior to this time most of the auditing had been done on the game: For each drawing the total amount wagered and the total of the winning pays were listed, and at the end of each shift these totals along with the cash balance completed the audit. Now there wasn't sufficient time for this auditing by the game operators, and it was done elsewhere by others.

On some games the writers took turns at the different duties, such as calling the game, punching the draws and checking the tickets. Several games operated with just two to five men; a few games were operated with only one man. When the volume of wagers became such that many writers were required, checking the tickets for winning pays became a full time job. On very busy days three to four hundred tickets (sometimes more) may be written on each drawing and two or more men may be required to check tickets and approve winning pays.

On some games it became customary to pay wins of up to about $5 from the customer's ticket rather than according to the original, because wins of these amounts were so numerous. This practice was convenient and, on busy days, it increased the efficiency of the game. This also made it very important to make accurate copies of all tickets, because a mismarked ticket gave the customer an advantage. If the original ticket produced no win but the mismarked copy did, the player collected and the writer never knew the difference. And if the mismarked copy produced no win but the original ticket did, the player still collected by bringing it to the attention of the writer who would then check the original and make payment. Some games paid wins in this manner in amounts up to $17.80, which was the amount won for a catch of 6 on a 35¢ 9 spot ticket.

This method of paying wins created a hazard from unscrupulous players that was not immediately realized on some of the games. It was not difficult, for those experienced, to alter a ticket which would create a win or increase a small win to an amount below $17.80. It has been said that two men in Reno each netted about $40 per day over a period of a few years, using this system. Some of these cheating methods will be gone into later.

The opening of new Keno games in the different casinos created, of course, a big demand for experienced Keno personnel. The clubs were able to train new writers within a few days prior to opening, but to direct and supervise this game requires a great amount of experience and knowledge, so the lack of experience caused many interesting events.

An incident, typical of the time, was experienced in a club after its game had been open only a few days. A 3003 way 10 spot ticket was played which caught 8 or 9 spots and no one working on the game could figure the amount of the win. The owners of the club had no idea what the win should be, so they took the ticket to the Palace Club game for assistance. These men figured the amount of the win, which was about $250. The winner was then paid and the game was immediately closed, and was not opened again until qualified personnel were found, which was *several weeks later!*

This condition created a situation of very little security for some of the casinos, which resulted in a reduced profit from the game. Wagers were accepted on invalid way tickets which were designed actually to change the odds to the player's favor. These were honest mistakes on the parts of some game managers who did not know the requirements of a valid ticket wager. This was the period of time when a few unscrupulous players used various methods to cheat the games of thousands of dollars each year.

Chicannery

On one occasion a cheat was thought to have been arranged in a most unusual manner. This happened on the graveyard shift in the early morning hours when only two men were working on the game, the manager and a young man who had worked on the game for only one month.

It was a slow winter night and a few hours had passed since a ticket had been played. The manager decided to go across the street to an all-night restaurant for breakfast. He told the assistant to write any tickets that might come in but to not draw a game until he returned. On his return the assistant informed him that he had written one ticket and, after waiting several minutes, the customer insisted that he draw the game, which he did. The customer caught 9 spots on his 25¢ 10 spot ticket for a win of $450. The manager did not question the incident because the customer was a member of the local police department, which at that time controlled the issuing of gaming licenses within the city; any accusation would have had the whole department down on them. So the "win" was paid. The manager waited a week before discharging the assistant. During that last week the assistant was, of course, never left alone on the game.

Cheating from within the game was done in many ways, most of which would not show up directly in the accounting. Some games were notorious for their chicannery against the house and also against the players. When a winning ticket was replayed without the player claiming a win, the ticket was marked "paid" and this amount was removed from the game's bank. Many times a player might overlook a win by checking the ticket with a wrong draw, and these small pays would often total $20 or more on an eight hour shift.

When a larger win (about $15 or more) was found in the book of original tickets and this ticket was not cashed while the next game was being written, a visual search was made for the party who had played it. (During those years the volume of write was small and the dealers usually remembered their customers.) If it was determined that this customer was involved elsewhere in the club and had not seen the results of the draw, or had left the club, all the draws for that game were picked up from the counter, then a draw of that same game number from the previous day was put on the counter, to replace the correct draw, for that player's convenience when he returned. A supply of the previous day's draws was kept on all the games, which, until a few years ago, was the custom. This draw would naturally produce no win, and the ticket was usually replayed and went back into the book of original tickets for the current drawing, where it was later stamped "paid." Customers were sometimes cheated of wins of more than a hundred dollars in this manner and this was not known to any one outside the Keno game.

On some games, because of security measures, it was not convenient to remove this money from the game's bank, so at least two game supervisors made other arrangements to collect. They conspired with the auditor and supplied the serial numbers of the larger unpaid winning tickets. On the following day, while auditing the game, he would remove these tickets from the book and cash them in, where they went back into that day's book as though they were then replayed. To prevent this, and other tickets from being inserted into the book, some clubs required the tickets to be stapled in the form of a book and one or two holes be drilled through the edge of each before the game was drawn. A ticket added to this book would then be conspicuous.

Most of the cheating done during this era was against the house and one such accomplishment was by inserting fictitious winning tickets into the book. Another by omitting tickets from the book. Omitting tickets from the book would result in a cheat of only the amount of the wagers on such tickets.

60

One man was known to use this system which netted him about $30 per day for several months. His method was to accumulate tickets (none of which produced a win) during the first seven hours of the shift, then go to the rest room where he shredded them and flushed them down the toilet.

It seems that most of those inclined to be dishonest are not content with these small amounts when there are other systems that would net them so much more, such as fixing a fictitious winning ticket. To do this, either the numbers that are marked on the ticket must be drawn or, after the draw, the winning numbers must be marked on the ticket. While both methods were used the latter was more common. This was accomplished by simply leaving the original ticket and also the duplicate copy blank until after the drawing and then spotting them as desired. This method was known to have been used by one game manager who marked seven winning numbers on a 35¢ 9 spot ticket, for a theft of $110.70 (less ticket cost) for each such ticket. He is believed to have fixed about four or five such tickets a week over a period of several years.

In the operation of some games this method of cheating in amounts of this size and smaller was accomplished by the game supervisors without an accomplice, and unknown to those working with them on the game. For large amounts, however, an accomplice was necessary and there is no doubt that many large winning tickets were fixed in this manner and paid off undetected. There have also been many such attempts that were detected before the payoff and some that were detected after the payoff. Some of these offenders were convicted on criminal counts. Others were fired and the matter dropped. In either case, they no longer have a future in the gaming industry.

One game supervisor was fixing fictitious winning tickets and dropping the duplicate copies to an accomplice in the basement through a short section of abandoned water pipe in the floor. It was not known how long this was practiced or how many accomplices he used, but when the scheme was discovered the accomplice was found to be a club employee in the security department who was on duty and in uniform.

Punchboard Keno

An unusual kind of incident occurred in Butte, Montana in about 1947. A type of gambling with punchboards had just been legalized (the duration was brief as this act was declared unconstitutional) and an attempt was made to legalize the Chinese lottery games, or at least make them more acceptable, by again fashioning the draw after the punchboard and calling the game Punchboard Keno.

The punchboard was a very popular gambling device during that era. Punchboards could be found in almost every tavern and coffee shop. They were made of cardboard and came in a variety of sizes and styles. The player paid five cents or more for the privilege of punching out a numbered slip in the hope that the number would correspond to one of the prize numbers displayed on the board.

For the Punchboard Keno game a board was prepared about one inch in thickness and about eighteen inches square, through which eighty holes were drilled in rows to resemble the form of the numbers printed on the tickets. Capsules were again used, and after the numbered slips were inserted into them and the eighty capsules were mixed, they were inserted one by one into these holes.

When the game was ready to be drawn one of the players, chosen at random, was allowed to select any twenty of the capsules he chose by punching them through the board where they were caught from behind in a container. The numbers on the slips in these capsules were then the winning numbers for that game. Each time a game was drawn the numbered slips from the previous drawing were reinserted into their capsules, then the other sixty capsules were removed from the board and all eighty were mixed together before reinserting them into the board.

This operation was in effect only six days when a scheme for cheating was carried out. It was thought that one of the writers, the one who was preparing the capsules and calling the game, conspired with two players in a scheme that went like this: In preparing the capsules for this particular drawing, those that were drawn on the previous game were readied by reinserting the papers and instead of mixing all eighty capsules together, the sixty that were not drawn were left in the board and those twenty that contained the last game's winning numbers were mixed and reinserted into the same holes from whence they came. All of this was done in such a casual manner that none of the four other writers on the game noticed. And none of the customers, except the two in collusion, ever realized that anything was amiss. When it was time to draw the game one accomplice was chosen to select the winning numbers. It was easy for him to remember which capsules had been punched out on the last drawing (or at least most of them) because the eighty holes through the board were drilled in the same relation to the numbers on a ticket. So most of these same capsules were punched out again. The whole scheme was so simple!

These two accomplices played tickets that were marked with only those numbers that had been drawn on the previous game. Several tickets were played, all of which were 35¢ 9 spots. Two caught all 9 spots for a win of $738 each. Three caught 7 spots for a win of $110.70 each, and others had wins of lesser amounts. The total of all wins was almost as much as the payout limit, which was $2,000.

One of the $738 wins was paid off. Then fraud was suspected and, after a couple of maneuvers by the management, was admitted to by one of the parties. The involved writer was then advised to get out of town, which he promptly did. Cage and balls were immediately put back into use for drawing the games; the punchboard has not been used since.

Money Recovered

When a winning ticket is determined to be fictitious after the payoff has been made, there is usually very little chance of recovering the money. An exception to this rule once happened after $12,500 was paid. A couple of hours had elapsed since the payoff when the casino owner, while examining the original ticket in his office, realized that he may have been cheated. His suspicion was aroused when he noticed that a small particle of ink in the edge of one of the spots seemed to overlap the ink of the serial number.

This date and serial number was stamped in the margin near the upper edge on the duplicate copy tickets, and on the original tickets it was stamped near the lower edge in the body of the ticket, as shown in figure 22. When there are spots marked in this area of the ticket the ink of the serial number may overlap one or more spots, because the tickets are numbered after they are written, but when the ink of the spots overlaps that of the serial number it indicates a possible fraud, because the spots may have been marked after the game was drawn.

The casino owner was not aware that his game supervisor was acquainted with the person to whom this money had been paid, but going on the assumption that a fraud had occurred, he called this supervisor to his office. The owner made no accusation but politely told him to phone his buddy and tell him to come right down to the casino and to **bring the money**. Such a statement as this would certainly indicate to the supervisor that something must have gone wrong, whereupon he confessed to the fraudulent scheme and phoned his partner. They returned $12,000 which was all of the money they had because $500 had been left as a tip to the writers on the game. They offered to work for the owner until this balance was repaid, but he told them no, they did not owe him any more money as he was fining himself $500 for ever having trusted this supervisor. No criminal charge was made.

64

An Educational Event

Many methods of fraud have been used. One which is noteworthy happened on a game which maintained an outstation. Outstations operate as an annex to the main counter and are situated at different locations throughout the casino. Communication between these outstations and the desk on the main counter is maintained with direct-connected telephones and two-way public address systems. At the close of each game and prior to the drawing, all tickets written on these outstations are sent, through pneumatic tubes, to the desk at the main counter where all the tickets are bound into books, usually a separate book for each outstation.

Immediately after the drawing of one game a request was made from this outstation to send back their book of tickets, that there was a question regarding a possible error on the duplicate copy of one ticket. The supervisor who was sitting at the desk was a young man who had been working in the game for only a couple of years and had just been promoted to this position. Having not yet learned the pitfalls, he returned the book to this outstation. This seemed like the proper thing to do because the party making the request had been his instructor when he started working on the game. The book arrived back at the desk within a matter of seconds, along with a reply that the question was cleared up.

Nothing was thought of this incident at first. Not even when a $25,000 winning ticket was found in this book, because the book had been away from the desk for such a short time. This winning ticket was a 9 spot and had been played for $10. It had caught 8 spots which was sufficient to win the limit. Of course the full story was related to the casino management, and trickery was suspected, but the ticket was paid off because there was not sufficient evidence to immediately prove fraud. However, within a few days a complete professional analysis of the ticket and the entire incident indicated that the ticket was originally a one spot and during the few seconds that the book was back on the outstation it was changed to a 9 spot ticket.

65

The writer who had requested this book on the outstation was discharged and the new supervisor, being innocent, learned a costly lesson at the expense of the casino.

Because of the possibility of a ticket being fixed in this manner, some casinos instituted a system whereby all original tickets, or a copy of each, which had a potential win of some set amount (usually about $5,000) would be deposited with the casino manager or some designated responsible party just prior to the drawing of each game. These tickets were usually given to a pit boss who would compare them with the drawing results before returning them. (Pit is the term referring to each group of gaming tables, twenty-one, craps, etc., located throughout the casino). These tickets were referred to as pit tickets, whereas today the term "pit ticket" is sometimes used when referring to tickets that are picked up by runners from players who are playing these table games. This "safety deposit" system was practiced for only a very short time and only in a few of the smaller casinos.

Balls Manipulated

It's practically impossible for the person drawing the game to have any control over which numbers will be drawn; however, there was some cheating done in the manipulation of these balls. The most common method was to hold out certain balls as they were returned from the display rack to the cage for mixing, and then during the drawing of the game return these balls to the rack as though they had been drawn from the cage. This method was usually practiced only on a small scale, but there was at least one occasion when it was thought that as many as eight balls were held out, creating a very large win.

Cheating, to be sure, has existed as long as gambling has been around.

The difference in the structure of games makes some more susceptible to cheating than others; it seems that the large-scale cheating that existed on some Keno

66

games during the 1940s and 1950s was a natural occurrence because of the attraction of the large amounts of money involved and the lack of security while the game was in its infancy.

A story related by a man who started working on the game in the latter 1940s shows how commonplace this cheating became. After two or three years experience he had just started work on a new job and was in charge of the game on the evening shift. One evening, within a few days after starting this job, the game manager came into the club with his wife and another couple. This manager came over to the Keno game and, while no one could hear them, told the new man to write him a 4 spot ticket. This mew man, not knowing what he meant, asked "A 4 spot ticket?" And the manager said, "Yes, a 4 spot, I'm taking some friends to dinner and need some change tonight. Give me $59 and write a 50¢ 4 spot on the next game." At that time $59 was the win for a catch of 4 on a 50¢ 4 spot ticket.

This new employee learned fast from the man who hired him.

There were occasions, many years ago, when the game manager would fix a phony winning ticket at the request of the casino owner. This was done for publicity. If the action on the game was very slow, the owner would arrange with some friend to present this winning ticket and collect the money (usually a few hundred dollars). A payoff of this amount was immediately known all through the club, and this always stimulated action on the game. None of this was ever known to the writers working on the game.

Just like the old days when the Chinese would sometimes fix a small win, in a manner such as this, on a player's ticket to stimulate trade from his neighborhood.

A Blower Type Ball-Drawing Device

In 1946 a new type of ball drawing device, pictured in figure 12, was introduced. This is a glass bowl with an opening in the bottom through which air is blown while drawing the game. Air turbulence mixes the balls within the bowl and forces them, one at a time as they are released with a trigger mechanism, up into the plastic tubes for viewing. The gates, located at the entrance of each tube, are closed to hold the balls in the tubes when the air stops blowing at the completion of each drawing, and are opened to release the balls which drop back into the bowl for remixing before the next drawing. This type of ball-drawing device is very popular and is used on the majority of the games throughout Nevada. This is true random drawing, like the hand cage, because the operator has no control over which balls will be drawn. This method of drawing has some advantages over the hand cage.

Figure 12. A blower type ball drawing device. Also referred to as a goose.
(photo courtesy Palace Club)

On one occasion, the first four balls drawn on a game using this type of drawing device were called as the corresponding numbers marked on a 4 spot ticket being played by an accomplice. This happened with two writers and an accomplice without the knowledge of three other writers and the game manager, who were working on the game right beside them. One of these writers was drawing and calling the game and the other was punching whatever numbers were called through the draws.

To prevent this type of cheating, a surveillance camera is used. It is usually mounted from the ceiling, several feet from the ball-drawing device. The camera is electrically operated and is actuated when the blower is started and again when it is stopped. In this way a picture is taken of the empty tubes before the draw and also one of the balls after the draw. Usually mounted within view of the camera is a clock, a calendar and a game-number sign which indicates the number of each drawing. This number sign electrically changes to the next number each time a game is drawn. These cameras hold a supply of film sufficient for two to eight weeks of operation; the film is developed when cheating is suspected.

Before the use of cameras some casinos required a third person to make a record of each drawing. This was done by noting numerically on a blank ticket the sequence in which the balls were drawn, and was referred to as a run-down. At the conclusion of each drawing this run-down was compared with the draws and the flashboard to confirm their correctness, and this run-down and one draw was filed as a permanent record of the results of each drawing.

Microfilm equipment is used on most games to prevent a ticket from being changed after the drawing, in order to fix a win. The original copies of all the tickets written on these games are microfilmed prior to each drawing. These microfilm units are electrically connected to a control system which interrupts their use during the drawing of a game. And when the blower is stopped the camera advances, leaving a short blank space on the film to indicate the completion of a drawing. These skips separate the tickets on each of the different drawings. A draw from each game is also photographed and this draw appears on the film next to the skip on the side with the tickets written on the next game. The security provided by this system lies within the electrical controls, which are always located so that they may not be tampered with.

On some games electrically-operated time recording devices are used in place of hand stamps for numbering and dating the tickets. This device dates and numbers the tickets serially as the hand stamp does, and some of these units also print the hour and minute. A few of these units print no serial number but show the time in seconds in which case the time is used as the serial number. In some casinos the electric circuit which actuates these devices is interrupted during the drawing of the games to prevent the numbering of tickets during this time.

When a ticket wins as much as some specified amount, usually about one to three thousand dollars, someone who is authorized by the management is required to verify the validity of each such win. The numbers on the balls that were drawn are verified and, in the case of microfilm equipment, the film is usually developed to determine if the ticket was photographed prior to the drawing. Usually, the payment of these wins is withheld until after the film has been viewed, which may require ten to thirty minutes.

Pencil Written Tickets

A system of producing a carbon copy of each ticket while it is written is used in a few clubs. Hard black lead pencils are used to mark these tickets instead of ink and brushes. The pencils are necessary in order to produce a copy through the carbon. The carbon copy remains in the machine and, until a change of rule was made, was the wager of record from which all winning pays were made. This rule was changed to make the player's copy (the copy submitted for play) the wager of record. This system is not very popular because these tickets are not as legible as those marked with ink. And the old rule which made the writer's copy the wager of record instead of the player's copy was not liked by experienced players because a mismarked ticket would change the intended bet.

The carbon copies of these tickets are on a continuous paper roll which remains in the lower part of the machine, secured by a padlock. This copy is examined in the event of a large win.

Game Procedure

The procedure of operation on different Keno games are the same in general — but vary in detail. While most table games use chips, Keno games use money for transacting bets and paying wins. (They will, of course, accept a house chip in payment.) The bank on these games consist of only the money necessary to transact normal business, which may be as low as a few hundred dollars on the smaller games and as much as $15,000 or more on the larger games. Money to pay large wins is drawn from the main casino bank.

Auditing is routine on all Keno games; each casino uses its own system of accounting, no two of which are the same. Some are quite simple while others are more complicated (most could be streamlined) but they all seek the same results — they determine the profit or loss produced by the game and also reveal any irregularity. An occasional loss on an eight hour shift is very common.

Just keeping the records for a game in the larger casinos is a full-time job for one or more people.

Some games stock numbered paper (blank inside tickets) from number one up to about number 250, and at midnight each night start with game number one, regardless of what the last game number may have been. This is the method that was used by the oldtimers from Montana and has remained the practice on many games since. Other games have changed from this method and they stock paper which is usually numbered up to about 300 and draw games through the last number before starting

71

again with game number one. The changeover to game number one can occur at any time of the day or night, which makes no difference, as there are never two games of the same number drawn on any one day. (This method prevents the fading from age of some of the larger-numbered papers.)

The average wager per ticket has increased through the years. During the 1930's it was about 25¢, in 1964 it was 68¢, about $1.12 in 1970 and in one club in 1977 it was $1.50. During the summer of 1978 in one casino on the Strip in Las Vegas the average wager reached $3.52. This was a Double Action game (two games drawn simultaneously); 46 percent of the tickets were played on both games. This creates a higher than usual average wager.

The amount of numbered paper used is about twice that of the unnumbered paper, which indicates that, on the average, each player's ticket is played twice.

When all tickets for a particular drawing have been written, the game is closed. This is the term used when the game is ready to be drawn and no more wagers are accepted for that game. It stems from the days when the counters were caged and each writer's window was actually closed during the drawing of each game. On most games the writing of all tickets are completed before the drawings begin, but on a few games those tickets that are in the process of being written when the drawing begins are completed while the game is being drawn. While the game is being drawn the numbered paper for that game is picked up from each writer and replaced with paper of the next game number.

Sometimes a wrong-numbered paper is put out and tickets are written on it before it's noticed. If this paper is numbered for some game in advance, then that game number is usually skipped and is not drawn that day; but if the paper is numbered the same as that of a game previously drawn that day, other procedures are followed. If the mistake is discovered while tickets are being written, the correctly-numbered paper is used to write the balance of the tickets and also to rewrite all tickets written on the wrong paper. The duplicate copies of the latter and those originals, which now bear two serial numbers, are kept separate from the others for easy reference. There were times when attempts were made to collect a win on such tickets produced by the correspondingly numbered previous draw. Very small such amounts were known to have been paid but a large amount has never been paid because of such error.

There have been occasions when some of the tickets were written on the correctly-numbered paper and some written on paper of the next succeeding game number. (This seems to occur mostly on games that have outstations when just one station uses the wrong paper.) In this case, with both game numbers being in advance, duplicate draws are made from the results of the next drawing, for both game numbers. This is done so as to have a numbered draw to correspond with the game number of all the tickets written. This one drawing then serves for both of these game numbers.

Draws also occasionally get out on a wrongly-numbered paper. In this case, new draws are always made on the correct paper and an effort is made to destroy all existing wrongly-numbered draws. If the game number of the wrongly-numbered draws is an advance game, then that game number is skipped and is not drawn that day.

Conditions such as these have caused only a few serious problems.

By mistake a player sometimes replays a ticket before the game is drawn for which it was written. He then unknowingly holds one ticket which is a receipt for two wagers. If the draw produces no win, this double bet probably will never be known. But in the event of a win in an amount that will necessitate the examination of the original ticket, the double bet will be known and the win will be paid accordingly.

Several runners (always girls, twenty-one or more years old) are used on most games. After each drawing these runners cover their designated areas in the casino, picking up tickets from those who wish to play. These tickets are brought to the game where they are written and the duplicate tickets are taken back to the players.

Sometimes a runner will arrive at the game too late to get a ticket in for a current drawing. The ticket is then written on the next game. If the previous drawing would have produced a win on this ticket, this sometimes causes a dispute from inexperienced players who, not knowing the rules, thought that the wager was in effect when the runner took their money. For this reason it is stated on most tickets that *"Keno runners are available for your convenience — we are not responsible if tickets are too late for current game."*

Many casinos operate two or more games, and to distinguish one from the other a different color is usually designated for each game, such as the "silver game" and the "red game." The tickets for each game are usually printed in a matching color. The game numbers also differ on each of these games. The draws on one game may number from 1 through 300, while the other uses game numbers 301 to 600.

These games operate with limits of the same amount.

The game number sign shows the number of the game for which the results are lighted on the flashboard. Above this number, on some games, is the wording "results of game." The number on this sign is advanced when the flashboard lights are turned off, just prior to drawing the next game. *(On the early-day games this sign showed the number of the next game, and above this number was the wording "next game." This number was then advanced while each game was being drawn.)*

The number of tickets written by each writer on the different shifts will vary considerably. With good action the average number of tickets written by each writer per shift will range from 1,000 to 1,200 and under ideal conditions can reach 1,500 or more. Of course, this fluctuates with the volume of action and with other factors.

Games that have outstations will sometimes average fewer tickets per writer.

It has always been the custom on Caucasian games to set a time limit for cashing a winning ticket. But the Chinese had no set time limit; a win of $17.80 was once paid six months after the drawing. This happened in Los Angeles during the 1930s. The player had left town before the game was drawn and no longer had the winning ticket and, of course, did not know he had won. When he walked into the gambling hall six months later the game manager recognized him and remembered his winning ticket.

Add Tickets

When a single player plays many tickets (usually 20 to 50 or more) on each game, they are sometimes put on what is called an "add." This is done to eliminate the necessity of making duplicate copies of each ticket for each of the succeeding games. All of the tickets are written on the first game they are played, and these original tickets are bound in a separate book from the other players' tickets. This book of add-tickets is then kept on the desk as active tickets for as many games as the player wishes to wager on. The duplicate copy tickets are usually also bound with a staple in the upper left corner for the player's convenience. A single ticket is now used on each succeeding game to record this wager, on which is usually written the word "add" and the amount of the total wager. Also a description of the tickets covered by this wager is noted; usually the amount of tickets involved and the starting game number. When several adds are running they may each be identified by a different number, such as add number one, add number two, etc. All of the tickets covered by an add are considered as one wager and this add-ticket is now treated as any other ticket wager. The total of the wins from all of the original tickets are paid on this add-ticket as one win, and when replayed it goes into the book of write as any other ticket.

An add-ticket may cover any amount of tickets; it could cover just one ticket. If a player intends to play a long way ticket for some period of time, he might arrange with the game manager to put it on an add to insure against it being mismarked during the play. However, such an arrangement for just one ticket is not commonplace.

Double Action Keno

In the early 1960s many casinos began to operate two Keno games and the thought of playing one ticket simultaneously on both games was conceived. Such a feature seemed desirable and a lot of thought was given to the idea. But before any such system could be put into operation there were many details to be worked out. A method of designating the game numbers to each game and showing on the tickets the numbers of the games on which it is played must be devised. Also a method of writing the amount of the wager on the ticket. And a system would have to be devised to synchronize the drawings of the two games and to close the write on each game before the other began to draw. These games were usually located quite a distance apart and to synchronize such an operation would not be convenient. Because of these complexities the whole idea was for several years only causually considered.

The first time that one ticket was played simultaneously on two games was in November of 1969 in the Club Cal Neva in Reno. These two Keno games were designed with this in mind and the plan was carried out while the club was being remodeled. Warren Nelson, one of the casino owners and a pioneer in the industry, designed the counters for these games and devised the method of play, which is known as "Double Action Keno." The counters were constructed and installed so that they each protruded from a common point, forming the shape of a loop so that both games could be supervised from one desk.

To distinguish between the two games, one was designated the "red game," the other the "green game."

The tickets for each were printed in a matching ink color. Drawings are made alternately between the two games and the red game draws only odd-numbered games while the green game draws the even-numbered games. In this way the game numbers that a ticket is played on are consecutive.

Figure 13A. Club Cal Neva's Double Action Keno game.
(photo courtesy Club Cal Neva)

When this operation started each game was operated individually (but the operation of both was directed from one desk) just as any other two games. A ticket could be played on just one game or on both, and could be started on either. The first draw for a ticket played on both games was always the next draw on the game where the ticket was written and the second draw was always the next following draw on the other game. The only drawback to this was that about ninety percent of the action was always on one game — the one that would draw next. So within a short time a change was made whereby all the writers would write tickets on the same game. The

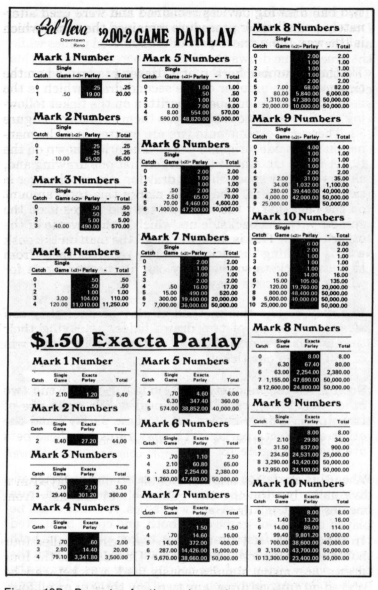

Figure 13B. Pay rates for the parlay and exacta bets.

78

two ball drawing devices remained and were used alternately and all other procedure remained the same, which is the way the games operate today.

The game number for the first drawing is printed on the ticket and the number of the second draw, which is the next consecutive number, is written on the ticket following the first with a dash between them as shown in figure 33. These same game numbers are written in a like manner on the inside (original) ticket. The price shown on the ticket is the amount of the bet for just one drawing and, as this amount is bet on each drawing, the total wager is twice this amount. The writer marks this total amount on the backside of the inside ticket and places it on the spindle with the backside up, which is the reverse of the other tickets. This is done to "flag" the man on the desk who is checking the tickets, and he removes these from the other tickets so that they can be checked again for wins on the second drawing.

The players like this method of play because they can await the results of two draws before replaying their tickets. Also because of the attraction of collecting a win of $50,000 on one ticket.

Soon after the innovation of Double Action Keno two other ticket wagers were designed which make use of two draws. One is known as "2 game parlay" and the other as "exacta parlay." The pay rates for these bets are shown in figure 13.

A variation of this original Double Keno is played in a few clubs by drawing two games simultaneously from two ball drawing devices.

In the summer of 1977 the Club Cal Neva installed four ball drawing devices on one game. On this game the four draws are made simultaneously and a ticket can be played on any one draw, any two, any three or on all four. A ticket played on all four draws could win up to $100,000.

Figure 14. Club Cal Neva's 4-draw Keno game.
(photo courtesy Club Cal Neva)

A feature of drawing four games from one goose, as suggested on page 24, has been considered by more than one club, and two methods of drawing have been proposed. One method would be to designate the first 20 balls as game number one, second 20 as game number 2, and likewise through numbers 3 and 4, completing each draw separately. Another method would be to distribute the drawn balls alternately among the four games. The flashboards would be lit accordingly — all four lighting up together.

Paying Wins

Large wins are sometimes not paid until after the next game has been drawn. These payments are often withheld for this period of time while the film is removed from the camera and developed and payment is approved. In the event there are other winners, the results of which may total more than the payout limit, all such wins will have been presented and the total payout will be known. On some games the books of tickets are not routinely checked for wins, in which case a win would not be known until after the player presents his ticket for payment.

The greater portion of winning pays are relatively small and these payments are promptly made upon presentation of the winning tickets. This is the **usual** manner in which wins are paid and is one of the terms that excludes this game from those defined as a lottery according to section 4421 of the Internal Revenue Code.

When the wins from one drawing total more than the payout limit, the total of the large wins are prorated to this limit and the smaller wins are always paid in full. Methods of prorating will be gone into later.

The prorating of wins is known to have occurred only a few times in the history of this game in Nevada, so it's not something a player should be much concerned with, 'though it could happen at any time.

40 Years of Keno

The casinos in Nevada have changed a lot during the 40 years that Keno has been played. Where the rooms were previously dark and smoke-filled, the casinos are now well-lighted, air conditioned and furnished and decorated to create an inviting atmosphere. Soft music is played throughout and almost continuous entertainment (stage shows) is common. The dealers are friendly. They show a genuine interest in behalf of the players. An incident typical of today's casino-customer relationship occurred a few years ago at a casino in Reno. After the drawing of a Keno game, a player was unable to find her copy of a ticket she had played. It was a 7 spot ticket and all seven of her numbers had been drawn. She knew which numbers she had played but had no idea what had happened to her ticket. She related this to the game manager who examined the original tickets and found that such ticket had been played and that it had won $5,500. Several employees began a search for the missing ticket and after some time one of the janitors found the ticket in a waste basket and the winning payment was made. Casino personnel are usually willing to assist players in any legitimate way.

81

Writer's wages are usually figured on a per-shift basis of eight hours, which includes lunch and coffee breaks. (One club operates with four shifts of six hours each.) In 1936 wages in Nevada started at $8 a shift, as this was the going rate in Montana. This rate gradually increased to $15 in 1946, to about $18 in 1951, to $25 in 1965 and to $38 in 1977. By 1978 beginners were starting at about $24 and within a year this was usually increased to about $30. The rate for experienced writers ranged from about $34 to $42 and for supervisors $50 to $75. The rate for runners was about $22 to $30. Wages are currently paid on a weekly basis; the total of all wages will run from seven to eleven percent of the total volume of wagers.

During the 1930s in Montana, wages were customarily paid daily in advance. That was so that the writers would be paid in case the game was closed by a police raid before the shift was over.

In addition to wages, writers and runners also receive tips (referred to as *"tokes"*). Runners' tips, like those of food waitresses, are usually in small amounts, but when a customer wins a large amount a tip of $50 or more is common. Writers' tips come mostly from players who have just been paid off on a winning ticket.

A winner of fifty to one hundred dollars might leave a tip of a few dollars and a very large winner (of several thousand dollars) sometimes leaves a tip of a few hundred dollars.

The tip is usually given to the writer who wrote the winning ticket or to the one who pays off the win. Writers' tips are pooled, then divided equally. Runners keep their own tips. On some games the writers' tips from all shifts are pooled in one common pot, but on most games each shift is pooled separately. This pot is divided daily among just those who are on duty on a few games, but a weekly split is more common, this usually being done on Sundays. (There were times in the past when the pot was so "slim" it was split whenever there was enough money to divide.) The amount received by each writer on most games today is small, perhaps $5 to $30 a week.

In Nevada a large percent of writers (perhaps a majority) are females.

Harolds Club in Reno was the first to use female writers, a custom which began during the early 1940s when there was a shortage of men because of the war. Until the early 1970s all-male crews were used on most of the games in the Las Vegas Area and on the games in Reno that were operated by the oldtimers who came from Montana. Many games employ fifty to one hundred writers and some have more than two hundred!

Keno's popularity has increased continually since the opening of the first game in the Palace Club, with the greatest rate of increase occurring since 1955 when the payout limit was increased to $25,000 and the "special rates" went into effect. In March of 1978 there were 122 Keno games operating in Nevada — the number of writers working on one game in a large casino was greater than the total of all writers in the State during the early 1940s.

Apprentices are continually starting and when there is only one or two they are usually trained on the game by an experienced writer.

When several beginners start together, classes consisting of about four to ten students are usually conducted. This happens frequently during the early spring of each year; the students are on the payroll and receive instructions for eight hours each day for about five days before starting their Keno careers. This has proven to be a very satisfactory method of training as this vocation is not quickly learned while working at the counter.

The amount of money wagered in 1978 on Keno games throughout Nevada is estimated to exceed $600 million.

CHAPTER 6

Mathematics

Devising the Game

All Chinese lottery legends agree that the game was originally devised and operated by the Chinese government for the purpose of collecting revenue. (It's referred to as a painless way of paying taxes.) They mostly agree, too, that the game originated before the time of Christianity, but no mention is made of how the probabilities of the game were originally computed or how it happened that one hundred and twenty numbers were originally chosen and later changed to eighty numbers. *It's not known when this change to eighty numbers was made, but this probably occurred after the thousand word poem was written, which may have been during the sixth century A.D.*

The arrangement under this new plan of using eighty numbers for the whole game, of which twenty are random drawn to create winning numbers and ten are selected and wagered on, seems to achieve ideal results in providing an extremely high-odds game of chance which also produces winners of smaller amounts in sufficient quantity to keep the game interesting.

These eighty numbers also adapt well to the poem from which the characters are used to make up the ticket.

A proposal was made in 1966 to change the game and use one hundred numbers for the whole game, of which twenty would be drawn. This proposal was not adopted because there seemed to be no real reason for it. The present arrangement produces odds of many millions to one which is certainly adequate for present-day use.

Under the new plan the first known reference to a ticket wager on any amount of spots other than 10 was made during the 1800s. The bets on these other tickets were first figured on the basis of the established 10 spot, and in essence each was a 10 spot way ticket. By 1900 all sorts of 10 spot way tickets, even the most complex types, were being played on some games. Most way tickets have so many different possible catches that it is not practical to publish the amount of the win for each catch, and not all players were able to comprehend some of these tickets.

Some of the more complex tickets were not accepted on all games, perhaps because the game operators did not fully understand them either.

Tickets containing fields of 8 through 16 spots, and also 12 spots which were divided into three groups of 4 spots in each (High-Low ticket), became known as standard tickets. And the amount of win for each catch on these was precomputed, at the existing 10 spot rate, and published.

In 1907 the minimum wagers on these tickets were:

8 Spots	$25.55	12 Spots	.65
9 Spots	.35	13 Spots	2.85
10 Spots	.10	14 Spots	10.00
11 Spots	.55	15 Spots	30.00
High-Low	.35	16 Spots	80.05

Early day minimum wagers.

These tickets were all, in essence, 10 spot way tickets with the same rate of winning odds.

At that time, and until the 1950s, the most popular tickets played were 9 spots, 10 spots, 11 spots and High-

Low tickets and, until the "specials" came out in 1955, the 10 spot was, by far, the most popular of all.

HIGH-LOW TICKET 35-Cent Rate Pays				
5 spots	2−2−1	pays	$	.20
	3−1−1	pays		.25
	3−2	pays		.30
	4−1	pays		.35
6 spots	2−2−2	pays	$	1.60
	3−2−1	pays		1.90
	3−3	pays		2.50
	4−1−1	pays		2.50
	4−2	pays		2.80
7 spots	3−2−2	pays	$	11.35
	3−3−1	pays		14.25
	4−2−1	pays		17.15
	4−3	pays		23.00
8 spots	3−3−2	pays	$	56.50
	4−2−2	pays		67.70
	4−3−1	pays		78.85
	4−4	pays		112.30
9 spots	3−3−3	pays	$	194.40
	4−3−2	pays		198.00
	4−4−1	pays		205.20
10 spots	4−3−3	pays	$	432.00
	4−4−2	pays		450.00
11 spots	4−4−3	pays	$	756.00
12 spots	4−4−4	pays	$	1,296.00

Figure 15. Ticket rates as played by the Chinese during the 1920s.

8 SPOTS $25.55 RATE PAYS		9 SPOTS $.35 RATE PAYS	
3 spots pays	$ 2.70	4 spots pays	$ .15
4 spots pays	39.80	5 spots pays	1.95
5 spots pays	271.60	6 spots pays	17.75
6 spots pays	2,578.15	7 spots pays	110.70
7 spots pays	11,386.80	8 spots pays	373.50
8 spots pays	31,266.00	9 spots pays	738.00
10 SPOTS $.10 RATE PAYS		11 SPOTS $.55 RATE PAYS	
5 spots pays	$ .20	5 spots pays	$ .60
6 spots pays	1.90	6 spots pays	5.30
7 spots pays	18.00	7 spots pays	42.30
8 spots pays	90.00	8 spots pays	207.00
9 spots pays	180.00	9 spots pays	585.00
10 spots pays	360.00	10 spots pays	1,080.00
		11 spots pays	1,980.00

Figure 15 (continued).

Shown in figure 15 is the published pay rate of these and the 8 spot ticket as played on one game during the 1920s. This particular game was operated by Chinese in Vancouver, British Columbia. This game operated with a $50,000 payout limit, and was the largest limit game to ever operate in North America.

Way Tickets

Illustrated in figure 16 is the method used in marking a multiple ticket. The lines are drawn to separate the spots into groups of 10 in each — so as to distinguish each wager — and the total ticket wager is apportioned equally to the groups, $1.00 to each. These are three separate wagers, each of which could be marked on a separate ticket, and are marked on one ticket only for convenience.

Figure 17 illustrates a simple way ticket. These three groups of 5 spots in each may be arranged, by using two at a time, to form three different 10 spot wagers of $1.00 each. This is also three separate wagers which could be marked, each on a separate ticket. The three ways on

Figure 16. Multiple ticket. This ticket contains three bets.

Figure 17. Way ticket. This ticket also contains three bets.

this ticket are easy to conceive by designating the groups "A," "B" and "C," and then visualizing each wager as being marked on a separate ticket; groups A and B on one ticket, groups A and C on another, and groups B and C on another ticket.

The amount of a win on such a way ticket is determined by the amount of winning spots that may be accumulated within any two groups, just as these two groups would appear when marked on a separate ticket. Should the drawing of a game produce two winning numbers in group A, four winning numbers in group B, and one winning number in group C; the accumulated winning spots would be 6 within groups AB, 3 within groups AC, and 5 within groups BC. According to the win schedule in figure 3 the catch of 6 spots would win $20.00, the catch of 3 wins nothing and the catch of 5 wins $2.00 for a total win of $22.00.

The notation in the margin of this ticket, just below the price, shows the method used to indicate that this ticket is played as three 10 spot wagers. This is referred to as "conditioning the ticket," and is necessary to show how the wager is applied, as this ticket could also be played as three 5 spot wagers, and the way it's played could make a great difference in the amount of the win.

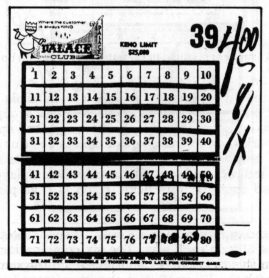

Figure 18. Multiple ticket with eight bets.

Dollar signs, cent marks and decimal points were commonly used in pricing tickets until about 1938. But these were omitted so that tickets could be written more quickly. The dollar numbers are now written in large size, the cent numbers are written much smaller, and instead of a decimal a line is sometimes drawn below the cent numbers when the ticket price is one dollar or more.

Figure 19. Another multiple ticket with eight separate bets.

Illustrated in figures 18 and 19 are multiple tickets marked with eight wagers on each. Each group of 10 numbers in figure 18 carries a 50¢ wager and spots are never marked on the numbers of tickets like this as they are not necessary. Figure 19 shows how spots may be used to indicate numbers that are not being played. The 8 marked spots on this ticket could also be played as such.

Illustrated in figure 20 is a 6 way 10 spot ticket with a wager of 50¢ on each way. The six combinations of 10 spots on this ticket may be visualized in the same manner as with the 3 way 10 spot shown in figure 17, that is by designating the letters A, B, C and D, one to each

91

group; the six combinations then are AB, AC, AD, BC, BD and CD. The catch on each of these ways and the amount of the win may be determined in the same manner as with the 3 way 10 spot ticket.

Figure 20. A popular type of way ticket with six bets.

This method of figuring the number of ways is a bit awkward on most tickets but could be used to figure the win and the number of ways on all way tickets of this type. A ticket marked with five groups of 5 spots in each makes up a 10 way 10 spot ticket, six groups make 15 ways, eleven groups make 55 ways, etc.

Way tickets may be marked with any amount of groups desired and each group may contain any amount of spots which can be so arranged to make up the desired wager.

Figures 21 & 22 illustrate two other methods of marking way tickets. In figure 21, the single spot (group of one) is counted with each group of 9 spots to make up the two combinations of 10 spots. And in figure 22 the 10 spot combinations are made up by counting the group of 9 spots with each of the one spot groups, one at a time.

92

Figures 21 & 22. Two types of 2 way 10 spot tickets.

Any amount of spots designated as a group must be isolated from other spots by the drawing of a line. The line designating a single spot as a group is always drawn

93

as a circle around the spot, as on the ticket in figure 23, and such a single spot is known as a king. The drawing of this circle is referred to as kinging the spot. Groups containing two, three and four spots are also circled, except when it's not convenient to do so, and groups of five spots or more are usually designated by drawing a line across the ticket, as in figure 20, rather than in a circle. The drawing of a line is referred to as cutting the ticket. These different amounts of spots are grouped differently just to make some tickets, such as the 8 way in figure 41, a bit easier to read.

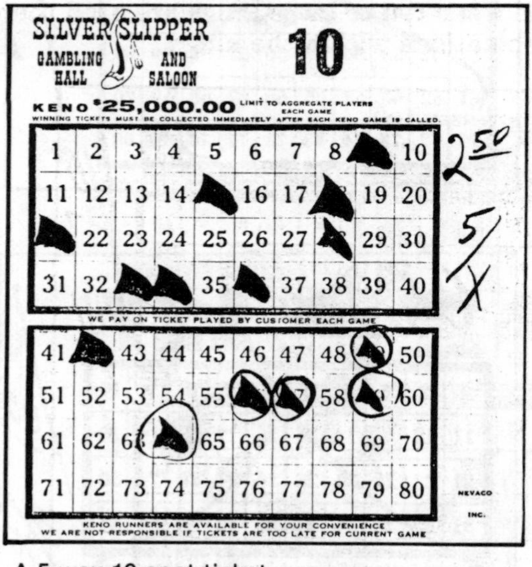

Figure 23. A 5 way 10 spot ticket.

Each of the five kings on the above ticket are counted, one at a time, with the field of 9 spots to make five combinations of 10 spots. The group of 9 spots on this ticket is usually referred to as a field because they may be scattered anywhere on the ticket. And any amount of spots used collectively may be referred to as a field. The spots within a field are referred to as pawns. A catch on the above ticket of five pawns and two kings would create catches of two 6s and three 5s on the 10 spot ways; that is a catch of 6 spots would appear on two of the 10 spot combinations, and a catch of 5 spots would

94

appear on each of the other three combinations of 10 spots.

The catch on each of these ways may be visualized by considering each way separately, just as if each way was marked as a single wager on a separate ticket. Consider just the 10 spots that make up one way and the catch within those spots, then the 10 spots that make up another way and the catch within them, and so on through all 5 ways.

Tickets like this are often played with varying amounts of kings, and when ten or more kings are used there are 10 spot combinations within the kings.

Figure 24. An 11 way 10 spot ticket. This was a very popular ticket until about 1950.

The field of 9 pawns with 10 kings in figure 24 make up eleven combinations of 10 spots. Each king is counted, one at a time, with the field to make up 10 ways, and the 10 kings counted together make up one way. This was a very popular ticket for many years and the field was usually also played as a 9 spot wager. The 10 kings make up ten other combinations of 9 spots but these were seldom played as such on this particular ticket. These 9 spot ways may be visualized by eliminating each of the kings, one at a time, and counting those remaining. So this ticket could be played as an 11 way 9 spot as well as an 11 way 10 spot.

Figure 25. An 11 way 10 spot ticket which was the forerunner of the 11 spot ticket.

The eleven combinations of 10 spots in figure 25 may be visualized, like the 9 spot ways on the previous ticket, by eliminating each of the kings, one at a time, and counting the remaining spots. The wager on each of these ways is 5¢, and a catch of 6 spots would win $5.10 according to the rate schedule in figure 10. This amount is derived by totaling the win from each of the ways. As each of the 5 spots that were not caught is eliminated, a catch of 6 spots results (6 out of each remaining 10), and as each of the 6 spots that were caught is eliminated, a catch of 5 spots results. Each 6 spot catch (five such catches) wins 90¢ and each 5 spot catch wins 10¢ and these total $5.10.

The win for this catch and all other catches on this ticket is the same as that for the 55¢ 11 spot ticket which rate is also shown in figure 10. This was perhaps the second wager considered to be a straight ticket offered by the

96

game. The 50¢ 11 spot rate shown in figure 10 is also the same as the 55¢ rate with each pay prorated to the 50¢ wager.

Figure 26. A 35¢ High-Low ticket. It was first played as 18-10s.

This High-Low ticket was also first played as a 10 spot way ticket. These ways are made up by accumulating all the spots within two of the groups plus 2 spots from the other group. There are six combinations of 2 spots within each 4 spot group, making a total of 18 combinations of 10 spots. Each of these 18 ways may also be visualized by eliminating 2 spots from each of the 4 spot groups (again six such combinations within each 4 spot group).

This became known as a High-Low ticket because of the difference in the number of winning catches produced by the difference in the distribution of a given ticket catch. For instance, five winning spots produce a catch of 5 on five different 10 spot combinations when two of these winning spots appear in one group, two in another group and one in the other group (a catch of 2-2-1), but if the five winning spots are caught, four in one group and one in another group (a catch of 4-1-0), a catch of 5 is produced on nine of the 10 spot combinations. The latter catch produces a higher amount of winning combinations.

This is the reason for the difference in the amount of each winning pay with a catch of the same amount of spots. It depends on how the spots were caught. This win schedule was computed on the basis of a 2¢ wager per way and was prorated to the 35¢ ticket. (See win schedule in figure 9.)

Until the 1950s the 35¢ 9 spot, as shown in figure 4, was the second most popular of all tickets. It was designed as a 71 way 10 spot. The 9 marked spots were considered to constitute a field, and each of the remaining 71 numbers a king, and the 71 ways are made up by counting each of the kings, one at a time, with the field. The win schedule was computed on the basis of a one cent wager per way (a 71¢ ticket) and was prorated to a 70¢ wager and then to the 35¢ wager. The first pay rate for this ticket was:

35-Cent 9 Spot Ticket	
Catch	Win
4	$ .15
5	1.80
6	17.80
7	110.70
8	373.50
9	738.00

Pay rate for original 9 spot ticket.

This rate of pay remained in effect until during the 1940s when the amounts for the 8 spot and 9 spot catches were increased, as shown in figure 10.

12 Spot Ticket

Since the mid 1950s the 12 spot ticket has not enjoyed its earlier popularity. Like the High-Low and the 11 spot tickets, this pay rate remained as that of a 10 spot way ticket after other ticket rates had changed, so that the rate schedule of these tickets was not as attractive as some of the others. (See pay schedule in figure 10.)

This ticket was first played as a 10 spot way ticket, and the 12 spots were considered each a group (12 kings), making a 66 way 10 spot ticket. The combinations of 10 spots on this ticket may be visualized by eliminating the two spot combinations and counting those remaining. And the accumulation of these two spots may be done in the same manner as described for counting the ways on the ticket shown in figure 20: That is to combine one of the spots with each of the others, one at a time, then one of these remaining eleven with each of the remaining ten, the one of these ten with each of the remaining nine, and continuing in this manner through the final remaining two spots. The catch on each of these 10 spot ways may be counted as each of the 2 spot combinations are eliminated.

The combinations on any way ticket could be counted in this manner, but as tickets get more complex a system used on the games for accumulating the count is more convenient. And this system of counting the ways and the way catches is quite simple.

To find the amount of spots caught within each combination of 10 groups (of 10 spots on this particular ticket, as each spot is a group) when 7 of the 12 spots are caught, we first determine how many of these combinations can be formed which contain the 7 spots that were caught. Each of these combinations will also contain 3 of the 5 spots that were not caught, so that ten such groups are written: 1-1-1-1-1-1-1-0-0-0. The 1s indicate the spots that were caught and the 0s the spots that were not caught.

All the spots that were caught are used in this arrangement so the only groups that can be substituted are the 0s. (There are five 0s and only three of them—three at a time—are used in this arrangement.) The total amount of 10 spot ways which contain a catch of 7 would then be equal to the number of combinations of 3 groups within 5 groups. And the number of such combinations may be determined by eliminating 2 groups in the same manner

99

as described for counting the ways on this ticket, and found to be 10. (The number of combinations of 3 objects within 5 are the same as 2 within 5 because when either is accumulated the other is eliminated.)

We next determine how many 10 spot ways contain a catch of 6 spots, and such an arrangement is written: 1-1-1-1-1-1-0-0-0-0. We are now making use of only 6 of the 7 spots that were caught and only 4 of the 5 spots that were not caught, so that now we have substitutes for both the 1s and the 0s. And the number of 10 spot ways which can be so formed is the number of 6 group combinations within 7, times the number of 4 group combinations within 5. The number of 6 group combinations within 7 groups may be determined by the elimination method and found to be 7. Also, by using the same method, the number of 4 group combinations within 5 groups is found to be 5, and so the total number of 10 spot ways which contain a catch of 6 spots is 7 times 5, or 35.

The number of 10 spot ways which contain a catch of 5 spots may be determined in the same manner and found to be 21.

There are no catches of any other amount of spots, and in practice the whole problem is worked out as shown below.

Groups on ticket Ticket Catch	1–1–1–1–1–1–1–1–1–1–1–1 1–1–1–1–1–1–1–0–0–0–0–0	
Catch 7	1–1–1–1–1–1–1–0–0–0 1 x 10	= 10
Catch 6	1–1–1–1–1–1–0–0–0–0 7 x 5	= 35
Catch 5	1–1–1–1–1–0–0–0–0–0 21 x 1	= 21
	Total	66

Computing the way catches.

The total of these ways prove that all 66 are accounted for, and a wager on this ticket of 5¢ per way would result in the following win, according to the win schedule in figure 10.

10 catches of 7 @ $9.00 = $90.00	
35 catches of 6 @ .90 = 31.50	
21 catches of 5 @ .10 = 2.10	
Total Win	$123.60

The wins from each way are totaled.

The price of this ticket wager is $3.30 (at 5¢ per way), and when this win is prorated to a 50¢ ticket wager, the win would be $18.73. The win for all catches on this ticket, prorated to a 50¢ ticket wager, is shown below for a comparison to that of the 50¢ 12 spot ticket.

Catch	10 Spot Way Ticket Win	12 Spot Ticket Win
5	$ .32	$ .30
6	2.59	2.60
7	18.73	18.70
8	106.54	106.50
9	374.09	374.00
10	912.88	912.80
11	1,916.66	1,916.60
12	5,000.00	5,000.00

Win rates for 66 way 10 and one way 12 spot.
Both tickets contain 12 spots.

This illustrates the simplicity of designing the 12 spot ticket from the 10 spot pay rate, which was also just as simple for the other tickets so designed.

The win of $5,000 for a catch of all 12 spots on this schedule may seem small when this is compared to the schedules of some other tickets in figure 10, but this is the result of using the 10 spot probabilities, rather than that of the 12 spot. A comparison of this schedule to that in figure 3 will show a relation to the difference in the two probabilities.

13 Through 16 Spots

The 13 spot, 14 spot, 15 spot and 16 spot tickets were designed and first played, like all other tickets at that time, as 10 spot way tickets.

Thirteen spots played as 13 groups (kings) make a 286 way 10 spot ticket, 14 spots make 1,001 ways, 15 spots make 3,003 ways and 16 spots make 8,008 ways.

These tickets, and also the 12 spot, were first played at a one cent wager per way. These are the prices shown on page 86. By 1930 the 16 spot ticket was no longer being played, and the minimum wagers on the 14 spot and 15 spot tickets had been reduced as shown in figure 9. The minimum wagers on these tickets were further reduced during the 1940s as shown in figure 10.

The 8 Spot Ticket

The 8 spot ticket was also designed on the basis of the 10 spot pay rate. The 8 marked spots were considered to constitute a field, and each of the remaining seventy-two numbers a king, and the combinations of two kings and the field make a 2,556 way 10 spot ticket. The win schedule was computed on the basis of a one cent wager on each 10 spot way, and the original minimum cost of this ticket was $25.55. In the early 1930s the minimum wager was reduced to $12.80 (one-half cent per way), as shown in the rate schedule in figure 10. When the game was brought to Nevada in 1936 this minimum price was

102

again reduced to $6.40 and on some games it was played for $3.20. The $2.60 rate (one-tenth cent per way) shown in figure 10 is a modification of the original rate and it came into play soon after the game arrived in Nevada.

These tickets, 8 through 16 spots, were the only ticket rates to be designed from the 10 spot, and until about 1930 were the only tickets played.

In designing these tickets it was not necessary to know the probabilities of the 10 spot as each of these was in essence a 10 spot way ticket, so the expected house percentage on each was approximately the same (just slightly more) as the 10 spot.

The 3 spot and 4 spot tickets were first played in about 1931 and these were the first tickets, after the original 10 spot, that required the computing of probabilities in order to design. At first these tickets wagers won only if all the spots were caught. The 3 spot paid odds of 45 for one and the 4 spot paid 180 for one. These tickets then carried a usual minimum wager of 25¢.

The 2 spot and one spot tickets were introduced in about 1933 and the 5 spot, 6 spot and 7 spot tickets were designed soon after the game came to Nevada.

For many years no one ever played a one spot ticket. *(There are Chinese people who have been playing this game for more than fifty years who say "anyone who plays a one spot is crazy.")* Until the latter 1950s very few tickets were ever played with less than 8 spots. The most popular tickets and rates played until about 1955 are shown in figure 9.

While the 10 spot remained the most popular ticket for many years these other tickets were designed to provide the players with a greater choice of wagering odds. And while these new tickets were being constructed the expected house percentage on most of them was increased about one percent over the 10 spot ticket.

Best Ticket To Play

Most players have at some time wondered which ticket may be the best one to play. With respect to the house percentage on each they are all about the same, but there are other factors that may be worth considering. The amount of the winning pay for each catch on all tickets is somewhat in proportion to the probability of its occurrence, and so the choice of which ticket to play might be determined by the degree of chance a player wishes to take as compared to the amounts that may be won. Listed in figure 27 are the probabilities of the occurrence of all ticket catches; a comparison of these to the amount of win paid for each reflects the approximate chance for the outcome of that wager.

All of the tickets, except the one spot and 2 spot, have more than one winning catch (some special rates excepted), and the accumulated probabilities of these winning catches for each ticket are listed in figure 28. These show the average number of times that each ticket is played before it produces a win, and this win may be any one of that ticket's winning catches. The 4 spot ticket is shown here to have the greatest chance of producing a winning catch and the 8 spot is on the other end of the scale with the least chance of winning.

A look at these charts will show that the amount of each win is proportional to its probabilities and that the best ticket to play is still a matter of choice. This applies to all wagers which have a potential win of an amount that is not greater than the house limit. There are methods of wagering on some tickets that will increase the expected win, which will be gone into later.

Probability of Each Catch Expressed As Odds For One Against Its Occurrence

Odds	Catch	Odds	Catche
1.3	0 of 1	4.8	2 of 4
1.8	0 of 2	4.8	2 of 13
2.3	1 of 4	4.8	4 of 12
2.3	1 of 3	5.5	1 of 10
2.4	0 of 3	5.6	2 of 14
2.5	1 of 5	5.6	4 of 11
2.6	1 of 2	5.7	3 of 7
2.7	1 of 6	6	0 of 6
3	2 of 8	6	5 of 15
3.1	1 of 7	6	5 of 14
3.1	2 of 9	6.7	2 of 15
3.1	2 of 7	6.8	4 of 10
3.2	0 of 4	6.9	1 of 11
3.2	2 of 6	7.2	2 of 3
3.4	2 of 10	7.7	3 of 6
3.5	3 of 12	8	5 of 13
3.5	3 of 11	8.3	0 of 7
3.6	3 of 13	8.8	1 of 12
3.7	1 of 8	9	4 of 9
3.7	2 of 11	10	5 of 12
3.7	3 of 10	11	6 of 15
3.7	2 of 5	11.4	0 of 8
3.8	3 of 14	11.7	1 of 13
4	1 of 1	12	3 of 5
4	3 of 9	12.2	4 of 8
4	4 of 15	13.5	5 of 11
4.1	4 of 14	14	1 of 14
4.2	2 of 12	15	6 of 14
4.2	3 of 15	15.6	0 of 9
4.4	0 of 5	16	1 of 15
4.4	4 of 13	16.6	2 of 2
4.5	1 of 9	19	4 of 7
4.6	3 of 8	20	5 of 10

Figure 27. Probability of each catch expressed as odds for one against its occurrence.

Odds	Catch	Odds	Catch
21	6 of 13	1,644	9 of 14
21.8	0 of 10	1,699	7 of 9
23	3 of 4	2,277	8 of 11
30	0 of 11	3,847	9 of 13
31	6 of 12	6,232	7 of 8
31	5 of 9	6,634	10 of 15
33	7 of 15	7,368	8 of 10
35	4 of 6	7,752.8	6 of 6
43	0 of 12	10,569	9 of 12
49	6 of 11	16,757	10 of 14
50	7 of 14	30,681	8 of 9
55	5 of 8	35,278	9 of 11
61	0 of 13	40,978	7 of 7
72	3 of 3	49,863	10 of 13
81	7 of 13	81,024	11 of 15
83	4 of 5	163,391	9 of 10
87	0 of 14	184,240	10 of 12
87	6 of 10	230,114.6	8 of 8
118	5 of 7	264,588	11 of 14
124.7	0 of 15	952,607	10 of 11
136	8 of 15	1,061,071	11 of 13
143	7 of 12	1,380,687.6	9 of 9
175	6 of 9	1,543,225	12 of 15
239	8 of 14	6,024,664	11 of 12
277	7 of 11	6,766,048	12 of 14
323	5 of 6	8,911,169	10 of 10
326.4	4 of 4	41,739,905	12 of 13
422	6 of 8	48,437,000	13 of 15
458	8 of 13	62,381,975.8	11 of 11
621	7 of 10	324,333,813	13 of 14
788	9 of 15	478,261,833	12 of 12
1,004	8 of 12	2,853,401,194	14 of 15
1,381	6 of 7	4,065,225,581.6	13 of 13
1,550	5 of 5	38,910,016,281.6	14 of 14
		428,010,179,098.3	15 of 15

Figure 27 (continued)

106

Average Number of Times Each Ticket Is Played Before It Results in a Winning Catch		
Ticket Spots	**Pays On Catch Of**	**Times Played**
1	1	4
2	2	16.6
3	2	6
4	2	3.8
5	3	10
6	3	6
7	4	16
8	5	48
9	5	25
10	5	15
11	6	41
12	6	24
13	6	16
14	6	11
15	6	8

Figure 28. Average number of times each ticket is played before it results in a winning catch.

CHAPTER

Counting The Ways

Way tickets is a method of marking many different wagers on one ticket. The way tickets previously illustrated are quite simple and easy to conceive but as they become more complex a system of counting is necessary to account for each wager.

Figure 29. A 36 way 6 spot ticket.

The amount of ways on the above ticket could be determined by the method previous explained, but a method used throughout the game today is more simple. This method is a mathematical calculation which, for the above ticket is $\frac{9 \times 8}{2 \times 1} = 36$. These 36 ways are the number of combinations of 2 groups (2 groups are required on this ticket to make up one way) which can be formed within 9 groups, and for the purpose of a short term this may be expressed as $C\frac{9}{2}$, meaning the amount of combinations of 2 within 9 (two-group combinations within nine groups). Without going into mathematical language, the number of groups which form one arrangement (one way) is written below the line (2 on the above ticket) and this number is reduced consecutively to one. The number of groups which the ticket contains (9 on this ticket) is written above the line and then reduced consecutively an equal number of times. This is now solved as a fractional multiplication.

This same method is used to find the number of ways on all way tickets and also to count the number of combinations within each catch arrangement.

Figure 30. A 56 way 9 spot ticket. Each of these 56 bets could be marked on a separate ticket.

Each of the 9 spot combinations on the ticket in figure 30 carry a 60¢ wager, and the use of 3 groups are required to form each of these ways. The short term expression for the combinations on this ticket is $C\frac{8}{3}$ which forms the mathematical calculation:

$$\frac{8 \times 7 \times 6}{3 \times 2 \times 1} = 56.$$

110

These fractional multiplication problems can easily be solved by the cancellation system, and the results look like this:

$$\frac{8 \times 7 \times \cancel{6}}{3 \times \cancel{2} \times 1} = \frac{8 \times 7 \times \cancel{3}}{\cancel{3} \times 1} = \frac{8 \times 7}{1} = \frac{56}{1} = 56.$$

For convenience, the short term may be used here and expressed in Keno language as $C\frac{8}{3} = 56$. This expression is sometimes referred to as "the formula."

Any way ticket can be played for all of its existing ways or it may be played for a part of the ways or various combinations of parts of the ways. In addition to the 9 spot ways on this ticket it could also be played as eight 3 spot wagers, as $28 - 6s$ ($C\frac{8}{2} = 28$), as $70 - 12s$ ($C\frac{8}{4} = 70$), and as $56 - 15s$ ($C\frac{8}{5} = 56$). Note here that the amount of 15 spot ways is the same as the amount of 9 spot ways. This is created by the fact (as mentioned on another example) that when either is accumulated the other is eliminated. This ticket is "never" played for all of these ways, but is often played for the 6 spot and the 9 spot ways.

Figure 31. A multiple way ticket. Fifteen tickets would be required to mark each of these bets separately.

111

A ticket which is often played for all of the existing ways is shown in figure 31. The conditioning in the margin of this ticket shows the typical method used to indicate each wager and how the total wager of $6.00 is apportioned. All 8 spots make one 8 spot wager of 60¢, the 6 spot ways ($C\frac{4}{3} = 4$) carry a wager of 60¢ each, the 4 spot ways ($C\frac{4}{2} = 6$) carry a wager of 30¢ on each, and 30¢ is wagered on each of the four different 2 spots. When all wagers are at the established minimum rates, it's not necessary to list the amounts of each, as is shown on this ticket. This was a very popular ticket during the time that the rate schedule in figure 3 was in effect.

All of the ways on a ticket such as this one are often played in the hope that if enough spots are not caught to win on the 8 spot wager, which requires 5, then a win may be had with a catch of fewer spots. The amount of the win for each catch on this ticket is shown below. Each catch is shown as the amount of spots caught within each group, and the wins in this schedule are based on the rates in figure 3.

4 groups of 2 spots	
1—8 @ 60c	4—6s @ 60c
6—4s @ 30c	4—2s @ 30c

$6.00 ticket			
Catch	Win	Catch	Win
1—1—0—0	$.30	2—1—1—1	$19.75
1—1—1—0	1.25	2—2—0—0	47.70
1—1—1—1	3.20	2—2—1—0	113.30
2—0—0—0	4.65	2—2—1—1	221.80
2—1—0—0	6.30	2—2—2—0	1,423.15
2—1—1—0	9.55	2—2—2—1	2,650.00
	2—2—2—2	$17,725.00	

Wins for all catches on ticket in figure 31.

112

The amount of the win for each catch is the total of the wins produced by each wager. The wins produced by the catch of 2-1-1-0 are; $3.75 for a catch of 2 on one of the 2 spots, $1.25 each for a catch of 3 on two different 4 spots (2-1 and 2-1), 30¢ each for a catch of 2 on two different 4 spots (2-0 and 1-1), $2.00 for a catch of 4 on one of the 6 spots (2-1-1), and 35¢ each for a catch of 3 on two different 6 spots (2-1-0 and 2-1-0), and all of these make up the total win of $9.55. The wagers which did not produce a win include the 8 spot, one of the 6 spots (1-1-0), two of the 4 spots (1-0 and 1-0), and three of the 2 spots. The wins for any other ticket catches are figured in this same manner; by breaking down the way catches for each wager.

Many casinos have established a minimum wager of 70¢ on any straight ticket but will write 2s, 3s, 4s and 10 spot wagers for 35¢ when the cost of the ticket is 70¢ or more. Also, some casinos will write any way ticket for a 35¢ wager on each way, and many will write most 10 spot way tickets for 25¢ per way and some 10 spot ways for 5¢ per way.

Figure 32. Another multiple way ticket.

Figure 32 is another very popular way ticket with the 9 spot and the 6 spot ways being played. The 3 spots are also often played on this ticket but a wager on the 12 spots is only occasionally made.

When a way ticket is not conditioned to show the amount wagered on each of the ways, such as the conditioning on the above ticket, then the total wager is apportioned to each of the ways played in equal amounts. This ticket carries a 60¢ wager on each of the ways being played.

A catch on this ticket of 3-2-1-0 (all 3 spots in one group, 2 spots in another group, one spot in another, and no spots in the other group) would produce the following catches and wins on each of the ways.

For the 6 spot ways, the catches on each of the 2-group combinations are arranged for counting and, beginning with the largest catch, these are written:

Group Catches		Way Catches	Win
3–2	=	5	$60.00
3–1	=	4	2.00
3–0	=	3	.35
2–1	=	3	.35
2–0	=	2	—0—
1–0	=	1	—0—

Reckoning the 6 spot wins.

For the 9 spot ways, the catches on each of the 3 group combinations are arranged for counting, and also beginning with the largest group catches, these are written:

114

Group Catches		Way Catches	Win
3–2–1	=	6	$30.00
3–2–0	=	5	2.00
3–1–0	=	4	–0–
2–1–0	=	3	–0–

Reckoning the 9 spot wins.

The total win on this ticket is $94.70. In arranging the group catches for counting, the larger group catches are written first in order that a system may be followed. It's common practice to omit writing the smaller group catches which do not produce a win.

When the ways on a ticket are made up with combinations of only two groups of equal size, such as the 6 spot ways on the above ticket, the catch count on each of the

Figure 33. An 84 way 9 spot ticket, played for 2 games (numbers 127 & 128).

115

ways is obtained by combining the group catches within each of the two-group combinations. This may be systematically done from memory and without writing the catches, by combining the largest group catch with each of the others, then the next largest group catch with each of those remaining, and continuing in this manner through all the groups, as shown by writing the catches for the 6 spot ways on the above ticket.

For those experienced in the game, this memory system is adequate for certain tickets, but as more groups are used to make up each way, the system used to compute the amount of ways on the ticket in figure 29 is used to count the number of combinations within each catch arrangement. The way ticket shown in figure 33 is a good example for illustrating this procedure.

This is an 84 way 9 spot ticket ($C_3^9 = 84$) with a wager of 40¢ on each way. Each way is made up of 3 groups, and the catch on each of these ways is determined by computing the amount of combinations within each group-catch arrangement. A systematic method for doing this is shown:

Counting The Way Catches

A catch on this ticket of 3-2-2-1-1-1-0-0-0 (the number of spots caught within each group) would produce catches on the 9 spot ways which are computed as follows. The arrangements of 3 group catches, beginning with the largest catch are written:

3–2–2	3–0–0	2–0–0
3–2–1	2–2–1	1–1–1
3–2–0	2–2–0	1–1–0
3–1–1	2–1–1	1–0–0
3–1–0	2–1–0	0–0–0

Group catches arranged.

116

The 3 group arrangements which total less than 4 spots do not produce a win, and are written only for the purpose of accounting for all 84 ways.

The total spots within each of the above arrangements represent an amount of spots caught within one or more of the 9 spot ways. Each of the ways is made up of one of these arrangements, and so the amount of combinations within each arrangement will determine the number of ways which contains each such catch. In practice this whole computation is worked out as shown:

Groups on ticket	3–3–3–3–3–3–3–3–3	
Catch on ticket	3–2–2–1–1–1–0–0–0	
3–2–2 1x1　　= 1/7	3–0–0 1x3　　= 3/3	2–0–0 2x3　　= 6/2
3–2–1 1x2x3　= 6/6	2–2–1 1x3　　= 3/5	1–1–1 1　　= 1/3
3–2–0 1x2x3　= 6/5	2–2–0 1x3　　= 3/4	1–1–0 3x3　　= 9/2
3–1–1 1x3　　= 3/5	2–1–1 2x3　　= 6/4	1–0–0 3x3　　= 9/1
3–1–0 1x3x3　= 9/4	2–1–0 2x3x3　= 18/3	0–0–0 1　　= 1/0

Way catches reckoned.

The arrangement of 3-2-2 produces a catch of 7 spots on just one 9 spot way, as this arrangement makes use of all such group catches $((C\frac{1}{1}=1) \times (C\frac{2}{2}=1) =$ one): there are no others that can be substituted. In Keno language this one catch of 7 spots is written in the form of a fraction, that is 1/7, meaning a catch of 7 spots on one arrangement, or one catch of 7 spots.

The arrangement of 3-2-1 produces six combinations with a catch of 6 spots. Within this arrangement the number of combinations of 3 is only one, as there is only

117

one 3 to be used. But there are two 2s to be used, one at a time, which makes two combinations, and with each of these 2s there are three 1s to be counted, one at a time, which makes three combinations. This creates the calculation of $1 \times 2 \times 3 = 6$, (($C\frac{1}{1}= 1$) x ($C\frac{2}{1}= 2$) x ($C\frac{3}{1}= 3$) $= 6$).

The arrangement of 3-2-0 creates a like calculation and produces six combinations with a catch of 5 spots.

The arrangement of 3-1-1 also total 5 spots and these groups make up 3 combinations, ($C\frac{1}{1}= 1$) x ($C\frac{3}{2}= 3$) $= 3$.

The combinations of all the other arrangements are worked out in this same manner, and the total of these combinations show that all 84 ways are accounted for.

Generally, this is the method used to find the catches on all way tickets, and when the total of these combinations do not prove correctly, one or more of the arrangements have usually been omitted.

Figure 34. A 252 way (deuce way) 10 spot ticket. This was once a very popular ticket.

Another ticket which well demonstrates this procedure is shown above. This is a 252 way 10 spot ($C\frac{10}{5}= 252$)

with a wager of 30¢ on each way. For a catch on this ticket of 2-2-1-1-1-1-1-0-0-0, the catch on each of the ways and the amount of the ticket win is completely computed and shown below. The win rate is based on that in figure 3.

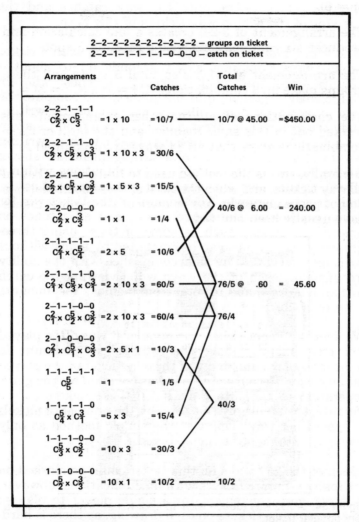

	2–2–2–2–2–2–2–2–2–2 – groups on ticket 2–2–1–1–1–1–1–0–0–0 – catch on ticket			
Arrangements		**Catches**	**Total Catches**	**Win**
2–2–1–1–1 $C_2^2 \times C_3^5$	=1 x 10	=10/7	10/7 @ 45.00	=$450.00
2–2–1–1–0 $C_2^2 \times C_2^5 \times C_1^3$	=1 x 10 x 3	=30/6		
2–2–1–0–0 $C_2^2 \times C_1^5 \times C_2^3$	=1 x 5 x 3	=15/5		
2–2–0–0–0 $C_2^2 \times C_3^3$	=1 x 1	=1/4	40/6 @ 6.00	= 240.00
2–1–1–1–1 $C_1^2 \times C_4^5$	=2 x 5	=10/6		
2–1–1–1–0 $C_1^2 \times C_3^5 \times C_1^3$	=2 x 10 x 3	=60/5	76/5 @ .60	= 45.60
2–1–1–0–0 $C_1^2 \times C_2^5 \times C_2^3$	=2 x 10 x 3	=60/4	76/4	
2–1–0–0–0 $C_1^2 \times C_1^5 \times C_3^3$	=2 x 5 x 1	=10/3		
1–1–1–1–1 C_5^5	=1	= 1/5		
1–1–1–1–0 $C_4^5 \times C_1^3$	=5 x 3	=15/4	40/3	
1–1–1–0–0 $C_3^5 \times C_2^3$	=10 x 3	=30/3		
1–1–0–0–0 $C_2^5 \times C_3^3$	=10 x 1	=10/2	10/2	

Way catches and total win are computed.

The procedure as illustrated is really very simple and adapts easily to all the different types of way tickets. The total win on this ticket is $735.60 and the total of the ways containing the different catches shows that all 252 are accounted for. This is the method generally used on the games to compute the way catches and the amount of the win on way tickets of this type.

The time involved in computing a win on such a ticket would vary from just a few seconds up to about a minute, depending on the ticket catch. Those who are sufficiently experienced in the game would compute the win on any way ticket, like the above type, by writing only the group-catch arrangements which produce a win and the number of combinations of each, without writing an expression beneath each arrangement as shown above. Knowing the number of combinations within a given arrangement without having to compute it comes only from experience. The amount of the ticket win for some catches on the above ticket, and all catches on many way tickets such as some of those using three-group combinations, can be computed by many without writing anything. This is accomplished with the ability to visualize each of the ways while viewing the catch through a draw, and to total from memory the amounts won on each.

When the 10 spot ticket was popular it was often played for any amount, above the established minimum, in multiples of 5¢, and many of the way tickets were played at 5¢ a way. Because of this it was common for the game operators to compute the win on these tickets at the 5¢ rate, then multiply this total by the number of nickels wagered per way. This was the simple method as only one pay rate must be remembered.

Each of the 252 ways on this ticket could be marked on as many separate tickets with no duplications, however, it's not very convenient for a single player to play so many separate tickets on each drawing, as there is hardly time to check each ticket for a win and replay them before the next drawing. This is another reason for playing way tickets. It accomplishes the same results in much less time and there is only one ticket to look at instead of many.

Way tickets may be marked with as many groups, and containing whatever amount of spots in each, as the player desires. When the groups are of equal size the number of ways is found by a single calculation, but when the ways are made up of unequal size groups the total number of ways may be determined in the same manner as shown on the above ticket for finding the number of combinations within the group-catch arrangements. Shown below is a ticket which makes use of groups of unequal size.

Figure 35. An 8 way 9 spot. This ticket was popular until the 1950s.

The 4 groups of 3 spots on this ticket make up a 4 way 9 spot by using 3 groups at a time together, and the field (group) of 6 spots is used with each group of 3 spots to make up four other 9 spot ways. An addition of another field of 6 spots would create another 4 way 9, making a total of twelve 9 spot ways, and tickets like this are often played.

121

Figure 36. A 12 way 7 spot ticket.

Shown above is a way ticket with the ways made up of one arrangement of unequal size groups. Each combination of 7 spots on this ticket is made up of one 3 spot group and one 4 spot group, which makes 12 ways (C_1^3 x C_1^4 = 3 x 4 = 12).

The catch on a ticket like this is written to show the amount of spots caught within each group size. A catch of 3-1-1 within the 3 spot groups, and 3-2-0-0 within the 4 spot groups, is written:

$$3\text{-}3\text{-}3 \quad 4\text{-}4\text{-}4\text{-}4$$
$$3\text{-}1\text{-}1 \quad 3\text{-}2\text{-}0\text{-}0$$

The group sizes are shown above, and the catch within each is beneath.

The catch on each of these 7 spot ways is determined by combining the catch on each of the 3 spot groups with the catch on each of the 4 spot groups, just as the groups are joined in forming the different ways. One method of joining these catches is to list the 3 spot group catches

122

vertically, and the 4 spot group catches horizontally, forming a triangle:

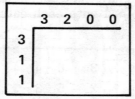

	3	2	0	0
3				
1				
1				

Group catches arranged.

Then as each number in the vertical line is added with each number in the horizontal line, these totals are correspondingly listed within the triangle:

	3	2	0	0
3	6	5	3	3
1	4	3	1	1
1	4	3	1	1

Way catches are reckoned.

These totals now represent the catches on all of the 12 ways, which are 1/6, 1/5, 2/4, 4/3 and 4/1.

Another method of joining these group catches which is often more convenient than the above method, and especially with complex way tickets, is to list each of the group size catches in individual vertical columns:

3 spot group catches	4 spot group catches
3	3
1	2
1	0
	0

Group catches arranged vertically.

123

It's now convenient to list the totals of each combination, and listed horizontally to the right of each catch in the second column, are the totals of that second column catch when combined with each catch in the first column:

```
3   3 — 6   4   4
1   2 — 5   3   3
1   0 — 3   1   1
    0 — 3   1   1
```

Way catches are reckoned.

This method shows the catches on all twelve of the 7 spot ways in a manner similar to the previous method. The catches which produce a win are one catch of 6 spots, one catch of 5 spots and two catches of 4 spots. Those that do not win are four catches of 3 spots and four catches of one spot. Either of these methods are equally effective for this particular ticket, however, as tickets become more complex the latter method is much more convenient, and is the one mostly used on the games today.

In writing the catches within the groups, they are usually condensed and written, in Keno language, in the form of fractions. As the problems get more complex, this saves writing the same number many times. Then in combining the group catches, the numbers below the line are added and the numbers above the line are multiplied, and these results are written, also in the form of fractions, as the catches on the ways. In practice the above problem is worked out as shown below.

```
1/3   1/3  —  1/6   2/4
2/1   1/2  —  1/5   2/3
      2/0  —  2/3   4/1
```

Another method of reckoning group & way catches.

The winning catches are now accumulated and the wins from each are totaled:

Catches	Win		Totals
1/6 @	245.00	=	$245.00
1/5 @	12.00	=	12.00
2/4 @	.60	=	1.20
	Total win		$258.20

All wins are totaled.

With a little practice this system is very efficient, and its advantages over other systems may be seen on the next ticket, which uses 3 groups in each way arrangement.

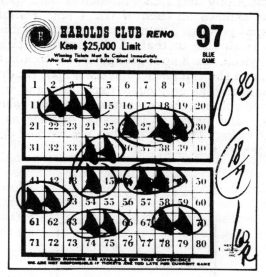

Figure 37. An 18 way 7 spot.

This ticket is similar to the previous one, but the groups of 4 spots have now been replaced with groups of 2 spots, and the 7 spot ways are now made up of one group of 3 spots and two groups of 2 spots. The number of 7 spot ways on this ticket is 18; the number of 3 spot

125

groups, times the number of combinations of two 2 spot groups. A method for viewing the combinations of an arrangement which make up these ways is to write the ticket groups in a horizontal line and beneath this the arrangement which makes up one way:

```
3–3–3    2–2–2–2
    3    2–2
```

Ticket groups and arrangement of groups making up one way.

It's now convenient to form the calculation: $3 \times 6 = 18$ ($C_1^3 \times C_2^4 = 18$), which is the number of 7 spot ways.

The catch on each of the ways on this ticket is determined by combining the catches on each of the 3 spot groups with the catches on each of the 4 spot combinations (two 2 spot groups). The method used to combine these catches is similar to that of the previous ticket. The catches within the 3 spot groups are written in the first column, and the catches within the 4 spot combinations are determined, as previously explained, and written in the second column; the catches in these two columns are combined and listed in the same manner as for the previous ticket. The way catches are worked out below for a catch on this ticket of

```
3–3–3    2–2–2–2
2–1–1    2–1–1–0
```

```
1/2  2/3  –   2/5  4/4
2/1  2/2  –   2/4  4/3
     2/1  –   2/3  4/2
```

Way catches are reckoned.

These catches are recapitulated and the wins from each are totaled to obtain the ticket win.

126

Way Catches	Win
2/5 @ 12.00 =	24.00
6/4 @ .60 =	3.60
6/3	—0—
4/2	—0—
Total win	$27.60

Wins are totaled.

This is basically the method used to accumulate the catches on all tickets which are made up of various sized groups. The way catches on any way ticket are counted by arranging the group catches in the same manner as the groups are arranged in making up the ways so that the catches within each may be counted.

The next illustrated ticket is similar in structure to the two previously shown, but with each way arrangement made up of compound combinations from two different sized groups.

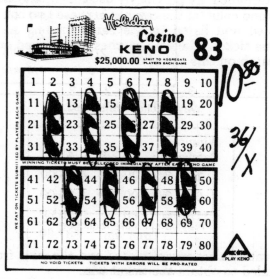

Figure 38. A 36 way 10 spot ticket.

127

The 10 spot ways on figure 38 ticket are made up from the combinations of two 3 spot groups combined with the combinations of two 2 spot groups (3-3-2-2), which total 36 ways ($C\frac{4}{2}$ x $C\frac{4}{2}$ = 36).

The catches on these ways are figured in the same manner as the previous ticket, except that the catches in both columns now are made up from their respective arrangements. That is, the numbers written in the first column are the catches within the 6 spot arrangements of two 3 spot groups, and the numbers written in the second column are the catches within the 4 spot arrangements of two 2 spot groups. The win is figured below for a catch on this ticket of

$$3-3-3-3 \quad 2-2-2-2$$
$$2-2-1-1 \quad 2-1-0-0$$

Ticket groups	3–3–3–3	2–2–2–2			
Ticket catch	2–2–1–1	2–1–0–0			
Way arrangement	3–3	2–2			
	Col. 1	Col. 2	Way catches		
	1/4	1/3 —	1/7	4/6	1/5
	4/3	2/2 —	2/6	8/5	2/4
	1/2	2/1 —	2/5	8/4	2/3
		1/0 —	1/4	4/3	1/2

Way catches are totaled.

Winning Catches			Win
1/7	@ 45.00	=	$45.00
6/6	@ 6.00	=	36.00
11/5	@ .60	=	6.60
	Total win		$87.60

Wins are totaled.

The catches in both columns are figured in the same manner as the 4 spot combinations on the ticket in figure 37.

When figuring the way catches on some tickets, three columns of catches will result. A convenient method for combining the catches within three columns is first to combine the catches within the first and second columns, and from these results, form a fourth column. The fourth column is then combined with the third column to produce the catches on each of the ways. Such a ticket is illustrated next.

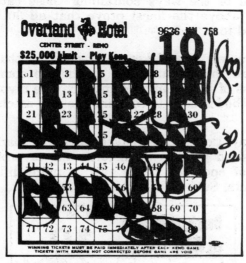

Figure 39. A 30 way 12 spot ticket.

Each of the 12 spot ways on this ticket are made up of the combination of one 5 spot group, one 4 spot group and one 3 spot group, making 30 ways (5 x 2 x 3 = 30). The way catches are computed below for a ticket catch of

5–5–5–5–5	4–4	3–3–3
3–3–1–1–1	3–0	2–1–0

Col. 1	Col. 2	Col. 3
2/3	1/3	1/2
3/1	1/0	1/1
		1/0

Catches of each group size are arranged in columns.

129

The first and second columns are now combined, and these results form a fourth column. The fourth and third columns are then combined and these results complete the problem, as shown below.

Col. 4	Col. 3		Way Catches			
2/6	1/2	—	2/8	3/6	2/5	3/3
3/4	1/1	—	2/7	3/5	2/4	3/2
2/3	1/0	—	2/6	3/4	2/3	3/1
3/1						

Fourth & third column catches reckoned.

The total of the ways containing these catches (the numbers above the lines) prove that all 30 ways are accounted for.

There are few way tickets played today that involve more than three columns of catches to combine, but regardless of how many columns may be involved, this same method is used to combine the way catches within them.

Many way tickets are played that are marked with various sized groups which form the ways of a given amount of spots by using two or more different arrangements. Such a ticket is illustrated next.

Figure 40. A one way 9 and 10 way 10 spot. A popular ticket until the pay rates were changed during the 1950s.

The single 9 spot wager on this ticket is made up of the 3 groups of 3 spots (3-3-3). The 10 spot wagers are made up of two different group arrangements: The 3 groups of 3 spots are used with each of the kings one at a time (3-3-3-1) to make up seven of the 10 spot wagers, and the 7 kings are used collectively with each of the 3 spot groups (3-1-1-1-1-1-1-1) to make up three other 10 spot wagers, making a total of ten different 10 spot ways that are wagered on.

There are many 9 spot ways and 10 spot ways on this ticket, other than those arrangements that are wagered on. The total amount of ways on a ticket is determined by totaling the ways derived from all arrangements which make up a given amount of spots. The amount of 9 spot and 10 spot ways derived from all arrangements on this ticket are computed below.

Ticket Groups — 3—3—3—1—1—1—1—1—1—1

9 Spot
Arrangements

$$\underline{3-3-3} \qquad = \qquad 1/9$$

$$\frac{3-3-1-1-1}{3 \times 35} \qquad = \qquad 105/9$$

$$\frac{3-1-1-1-1-1-1}{3 \times 7} \qquad = \qquad \underline{21/9}$$

Total 9 spot ways $\qquad = 127$

10 Spot
Arrangements

$$\frac{3-3-3-1}{1 \times 7} \qquad = \qquad 7/10$$

$$\frac{3-3-1-1-1-1}{3 \times 35} \qquad = \qquad 105/10$$

$$\frac{3-1-1-1-1-1-1-1}{3 \times 1} \qquad = \qquad \underline{3/10}$$

Total 10 spot ways $\qquad = 115$

9 and 10 spot way computed.

131

Even though there are more ways on this ticket than are being played, this is a valid ticket wager, because there are no conflicting arrangements which will produce the same amount of ways as those that are being played.

Ticket of Many Wagers

In reviewing tickets, it's only appropriate to mention the old "8 way," which was perhaps the most popular of all way tickets until the rates were changed during the 1950s.

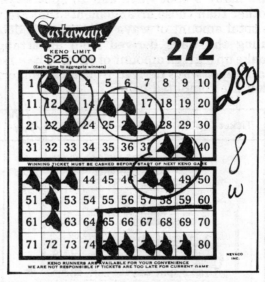

Figure 41. The old 8 way. A very popular early-day ticket.

The conditioning on this ticket is unusual, and it means that 8 ways are being played, each at a 35¢ wager. These 8 ways consist of one 10 spot (5-5), one High-Low (4-4-4), and six 9 spots (5-4). There are other ways (containing other amount of spots, such as 8 and 14) on this ticket, but at the time it was first played these were the only ways that could be played for a wager as small as 35¢; and the illustrated conditioning became standard for this ticket. (The practice of circling groups containing 4 spots or less and cutting groups of 5 spots or more originated on this ticket. This method of separating the spots distinguishes the group sizes better.)

132

When this ticket was first played, the High-Low and the 9 spot wagers were, in essence, 10 spot ways, and so this ticket actually contained 445 separate wagers, 10 spots in each, each of which could be marked on a separate ticket with no duplications. (Each 9 spot contained 71 ways and the High-Low contained 18 ways.)

A ticket marked with 3 groups of 4 spots in each and one group (field) of 5 spots was played (and, like the 8 way, is still played in some clubs) as a "4 way" for a 35¢ wager on each way. These ways are one High-Low and three 9 spots.

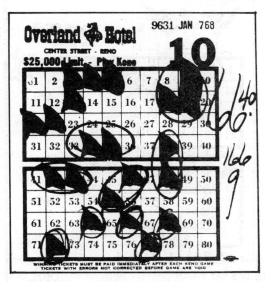

Figure 42. A 166 way 9 spot ticket. This ticket was rarely played.

Shown above is a ticket with the 9 spot ways of all arrangements being played. Each of these ways carry a 40¢ wager, and are made up of several different arrangements.

While a ticket like this is being played, the game manager or the party who is checking the tickets for wins, usually makes a list of the arrangements that are being played, to be used as a quick reference in checking the ticket.

133

Each of these arrangements are listed below, along with the number of ways within each.

Ticket Groups
6–3–2–2–2–2–1–1–1–1–1

Arrangements		Ways
$\dfrac{6-3}{1 \times 1}$	=	1/9
$\dfrac{6-2-1}{1 \times 4 \times 5}$	=	20/9
$\dfrac{6-1-1-1}{1 \times 10}$	=	10/9
$\dfrac{3-2-2-2}{1 \times 4}$	=	4/9
$\dfrac{3-2-2-1-1}{1 \times 6 \times 10}$	=	60/9
$\dfrac{3-2-1-1-1-1}{1 \times 4 \times 5}$	=	20/9
$\dfrac{2-2-2-2-1}{1 \times 5}$	=	5/9
$\dfrac{2-2-2-1-1-1}{4 \times 10}$	=	40/9
$\dfrac{2-2-1-1-1-1-1}{6 \times 1}$	=	6/9
Total 9 spot ways	=	**166**

Ways computed for all 9 spot arrangements.

In figuring the way catches on a ticket like this, each arrangement is considered individually. The way catches are figured below for a ticket catch of

6–3–2–2–2–2–1–1–1–1–1
3–2–2–2–0–0–1–1–0–0–0

Arrangement Catches		9 Spot Way Catches		
6–3				
1/3 1/2		– 1/5		
6–2–1	(*)			
1/3 2/2 2/1	2/5	– 4/6	6/5	
2/0 3/0	2/3	– 4/4	6/3	
6–1–1–1				
1/3 3/2		– 3/5		
6/1		– 6/4		
1/0		– 1/3		
3–2–2–2				
1/2 2/4		– 2/6		
2/2		– 2/4		
3–2–2–1–1	(*)			
1/2 1/4 1/2	1/6	– 1/8	6/7	3/6
4/2 6/1	4/4	– 4/6	24/5	12/4
1/0 3/0	1/2	– 1/4	6/3	3/2
3–2–1–1–1–1	(*)			
1/2 2/2 3/2	2/4	– 6/6	4/5	
2/0 2/1	2/2	– 6/4	4/3	
2–2–2–2–1				
1/4 2/1		– 2/5		
3/0		– 3/4		
2–2–2–1–1–1				
2/4 3/2		– 6/6	6/4	
2/2 6/1		– 12/5	12/3	
1/0		– 2/4	2/2	
2–2–1–1–1–1–1				
1/4 1/2		– 1/6	4/4	1/2
4/2				
1/0				

9 spot way catches computed.

Three of these arrangements create three columns of catches to be combined, and the first and second columns of these arrangements are combined to create a fourth column (*), which is combined with the third

135

column to complete the computation of these combinations.

The catches on all 166 ways are accounted for; and shown below, the winning catches of each arrangement are accumulated and the amounts won on each are totaled for the ticket win.

Arrangements	Catch				Win	
6–3	1/5	@	2.00	=	$	2.00
6–2–1	4/6	@	18.00	=		72.00
	6/5	@	2.00	=		12.00
	4/4	@	.20	=		.80
6–1–1–1	3/5	@	2.00	=		6.00
	6/4	@	.20	=		1.20
3–2–2–2	2/6	@	18.00	=		36.00
	2/4	@	.20	=		.40
3–2–2–1–1	1/8	@	1,100.00	=		1,100.00
	6/7	@	112.00	=		672.00
	7/6	@	18.00	=		126.00
	24/5	@	2.00	=		48.00
	13/4	@	.20	=		2.60
3–2–1–1–1–1	6/6	@	18.00	=		108.00
	4/5	@	2.00	=		8.00
	6/4	@	.20	=		1.20
2–2–2–2–1	2/5	@	2.00	=		4.00
	3/4	@	.20	=		.60
2–2–2–1–1–1	6/6	@	18.00	=		108.00
	12/5	@	2.00	=		24.00
	8/4	@	.20	=		1.60
2–2–1–1–1–1–1	1/6	@	18.00	=		18.00
	4/4	@	.20	=		.80

The ticket win is figured.

The total ticket win is now obtained by adding the figures in the win column.

This ticket could be played for any portion of these 9 spot arrangements which total an amount of ways that do not coincide with the amount of ways produced by other arrangements; or by conditioning the ticket to indicate which arrangement is being played, as illustrated on the ticket below, any one or more arrangements could be played.

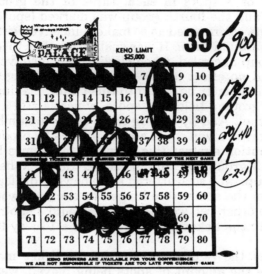

Figure 43. A multiple way ticket played as a 170 way 10 spot and as a 20 way 9 spot.

All arrangements of 10 spot ways in figure 43 are now played, but the only 9 spot ways that are wagered on is the one arrangement of 6-2-1 as indicated. The ways of other amounts of spots could also be played.

When a student of the game is familiar with the procedure for computing the win on tickets such as these, then the amount of ways and the way catches may logically be reasoned for any Keno ticket.

Conditioning Tickets

When all wins were paid according to the original ticket (on some games they were always so paid) it made little difference what fashion was used in writing the duplicate copies. But when it became the custom to pay small wins from these duplicate copies, some players were quick to take advantage of the game by altering their tickets to produce or increase a small win.

A 4 way 9 spot was an easy ticket to change, and it was often played for that purpose. It was marked with 4 groups of 3 spots in each; three of the groups were circled and the fourth group was marked (spotted) with the spots so arranged as to make it inconvenient to draw a circle around them. It was customary then to leave this one group uncircled, when circling was inconvenient, as this had no effect on the validity of the wager. But 3 spots could later be added to this ticket, making the un-circled group a field of 6 spots, which is still a 4 way 9 spot ticket. And by adding these spots to numbers that were drawn, a win could almost always be produced. As a precaution against this, some of the games began to circle all groups on this particular ticket. When one of the groups was so scattered as to be very difficult to cir-cle, then the spots were kinged or one spot was kinged and the other two were grouped. Should 3 spots then be added to the ticket it would become a 10 way 9 spot.

Some of the figures written in the ticket margin, to indicate the amount of spots being played, were easily changed, and by changing this figure it was easy to pro-duce a win. A 50¢ 4 spot ticket was once changed in this manner to produce a win. A figure "1" was written in front of the 4, and 10 spots were added to make a 14 spot ticket. This ticket was presented to a writer for payment with a catch of 9 spots for a win of $197. The player, ap-parently inexperienced, didn't know that wins of this amount were paid according to the original ticket!

To prevent changes such as these a method of condition-ing tickets was adapted by some clubs. For the one spot, the word "one" was usually written, either in the margin or was begun in the body of the ticket and finished in the margin. The numerals were written and circled, or half-circled, on 2 spot, 3 spot, 4 spot, 5 spot and ll spot tickets and sometimes on 7 spot tickets as these numerals are the most easily changed. Then if a circled 14 spot ticket

138

is presented with a win (even a very small win), it is always paid from the original ticket, as it may have been a 4 spot and changed to a 14 spot.

When tickets are played for a wager that is a multiple of two or more pay rates, the rate being played is indicated in the margin. There are usually only two different pay rates for each ticket and these are known as "regular" or "special." The absence of any notation indicates the regular rate is being played and for the special rate an "S" is written in the margin near the bottom of the ticket.

Figure 10 lists the 15 spot ticket at a 50¢ rate, which begins to pay on a catch of 7 or more spots, and a $1.50 rate, which begins to pay on a catch of 5 or more spots. If this ticket was played for $1.50 or any multiple thereof, then a notation was made to indicate which rate was being played: "P5" (pay on 5) for the $1.50 rate and "P7" for the 50¢ rate.

A $4.95 wager on the 9 spot ticket is a multiple of the 45¢ rate and also the 55¢ rate (both shown in figure 10), and both of these began to pay on a catch of 5 or more spots. So on this ticket the notations "45R" and "55R" was used to indicate the rate.

CHAPTER

Probabilities

The probability of an event's occurrence is a ratio of its likeliness to that of its unlikeliness, and may be expressed in several different ways, such as a fraction, or as a percentage, or as odds. The probabilities of many gambling events are expressed as odds against its occurrence; these odds may be expressed in two different ways, either "for" or "to." Odds of five to one against the occurrence of an event means that out of six attempts the event is expected to occur once. This same ratio, when the odds are expressed as "for," is six for one. When the winning odds are expressed as five to one, a winning bettor receives five dollars for a one dollar wager plus the amount wagered, or six dollars. When this same ratio is expressed as odds of five for one, a winning bettor receives five dollars for a one dollar wager and loses the amount wagered. The amount of the win is the same with either method of expressing odds.

It's convenient to express a ratio as "odds to" in many gambling events. This is the usual method on most table games, such as a dice table, because the results of the wagers are usually so soon known and the owners of each bet are also known, as all participants are present during each event. When the probabilities or the win ratios of Keno are expressed as odds, they are always expressed as "for," as this is more practical in this type of event.

The probabilities of Keno are much more tedious to compute than those of most gambling events, but the task is accomplished in the same general manner — that is, to compare the totals of all the possible outcomes. The ratio of the outcomes resulting from the total possible different wagers of a given ticket played on one drawing will indicate the probabilities of a single wager on that ticket.

One Spot Probabilities

The probabilities of the one spot ticket are simple to figure. The total possible different wagers is eighty; and if these eighty tickets are played on one drawing, twenty of them will win and sixty of them will lose. Twenty of the eighty numbers are drawn each game, and so twenty of these tickets must win and sixty of them must lose. This win ratio is one in four ($\frac{20}{80}$ = ¼), which means that out of each four tickets played, one of them is expected to win. This ratio could be expressed as a one-fourth chance of winning, a twenty-five percent chance of winning, or odds of four for one against winning. This expectation is the same whether four tickets are played on one game or one ticket is played on four games or any other arrangement.

The win rate for this ticket is three for one (a 60¢ wager wins $1.80); and so out of each four wagers made, one of them is expected to win; and the amount of this win is equal to the cost of three wagers. So then seventy-five percent of all monies wagered on the one spot ticket is expected to be paid out in wins.

Because the probabilities of the one spot ticket are in even numbers, it is easy to compute the percentage as shown. The probabilities of other tickets, if reduced to a ratio equal to one, are in long decimal fractions; and so, instead of reducing the ratio, it's just as convenient to work with the large whole numbers.

2 Spot Probabilities

For the 2 spot ticket there are 3,160 possible different wagers ($C\frac{80}{2}$ = 3,160), and when all of these tickets are played on one drawing 190 of them must win. This is the number of 2 spot combinations within the 20 drawn numbers; $C\frac{20}{2}$ = 190. The tickets which lose are those that catch one spot and those that catch no spots.

The amount of tickets that catch one spot is 1,200. One of the spots on each of these tickets must be one of the twenty numbers that were drawn, and the other spot must be one of the sixty numbers that were not drawn; and so the amount of such combinations is 20 times 60, which equals 1,200.

The tickets that catch no spots are all marked within the sixty numbers that were not drawn, and so the amount of these tickets are the number of combinations of 2 within 60, which equals 1,770 (C_2^{60} = 1,770).

In figuring the probabilities of a Keno ticket, it is not necessary to determine the amount of losing tickets; however, this is a method of checking the finished work. The total of tickets from all catches must equal the amount of the possible different wagers.

The amount expected to be paid out in wins on the 2 spot ticket is 75.1 percent of the amount wagered. This is determined by dividing the amount wagered on the total possible different tickets (3,160 x 60¢) into the amount of the wins paid out (190 x $7.50).

This same procedure is used to figure the percentage probability of all tickets. Of the total possible different wagers on a given ticket, the amount of such tickets which have a winning catch is determined. The amounts paid out for these winning catches are totaled, and this figure is divided by the total amount wagered, and this product is the percentage of the monies wagered which is expected to be paid out in wins. Finding the prob-- abilities of the 6 spot ticket, which has four winning catches, will illustrate this full procedure.

6 Spot Probabilities

The total amount of 6 spot tickets which are each different from the other is the amount of combinations of 6 within 80, which is 300,500,200 (C_6^{80} = 300,500,200). If 60¢ is wagered on each of these tickets, the total amount wagered is $180,300,120.00.

The amount of these tickets that catch all 6 spots is the number of combinations of 6 within 20, which is 38,760 (C_6^{20} = 38,760). For a 60¢ wager, each of these tickets will win $1,250.00 for a total payout of $48,450,000.00.

143

The amount of tickets that catch 5 spots is the amount of combinations of 5 within 20, times the number of combinations of one within 60, which is 930,240 ($C \frac{20}{5}$ x $C \frac{60}{1}$ = 930,240). Each of these tickets win $60.00 for a total payout of $55,814,400.00.

The amount of tickets that catch 4 spots is the number of combinations of 4 within 20, times the number of combinations of 2 within 60, which is 8,575,650 ($C \frac{20}{4}$ x $C \frac{60}{2}$ = 8,575,650). Each of these tickets win $2.00 for a total payout of $17,151,300.00.

The amount of tickets that catch 3 spots is the number of combinations of 3 within 20, times the number of combinations of 3 within 60, which is 39,010,800 ($C \frac{20}{3}$ x $C \frac{60}{3}$ = 39,010,800). Each of these tickets win 35¢ for a total payout of $13,653,780.00. (It's amazing how many dollars are paid out at 35¢ per pay.)

The total of all of these winning pays is $135,069,480.00, and when this figure is divided by the total amount wagered, it shows that 74.913 percent is paid out in wins.

Combinations

The most tedious part of computing the outcomes of Keno events is figuring the various combinations, and even then the figures to be multiplied, to find the amount of each arrangement, are often many digits, requiring a lot of time to compute.

For example, to find the amount of 14 spot tickets, out of the total possible 14 spot combinations, which would produce a catch of 5 spots, the calculation would be $C \frac{20}{5}$ x $C \frac{60}{9}$, and when this is written out to begin the computation it looks like this:

$$\left(\frac{20 \times 19 \times 18 \times 17 \times 16}{5 \times 4 \times 3 \times 2 \times 1}\right) \times \left(\frac{60 \times 59 \times 58 \times 57 \times 56 \times 55 \times 54 \times 53 \times 52}{9 \times 8 \times 7 \times 6 \times 5 \times 4 \times 3 \times 2 \times 1}\right)$$

The number of combinations of 5 within 20 is 15,504, and the number of combinations of 9 within 60 is 14,783,142,660; when multiplied the answer is 229,197,843,800,640.

144

For convenience in designing ticket pay rates, these combinations of numbers up to 20 within twenty, sixty and eighty, are shown in figures 44, 45 and 46 respectively. Figure 47 shows these combinations within forty, which are used to find other probabilities.

The outcome for each ticket (the amount of tickets which produce each catch), when the total of the combinations of each are played on one drawing, is shown in figure 48.

Combinations within 20			
1	20	11	167,960
2	190	12	125,970
3	1,140	13	77,520
4	4,845	14	38,760
5	15,504	15	15,504
6	38,760	16	4,845
7	77,520	17	1,140
8	125,970	18	190
9	167,960	19	20
10	184,756	20	1

Figure 44. Amount of group combinations within 20 groups.

Combinations within 60			
1	60	11	342,700,125,300
2	1,770	12	1,399,358,844,975
3	34,220	13	5,166,863,427,600
4	487,635	14	17,345,898,649,800
5	5,461.512	15	53,194,089,192,720
6	50,063,860	16	149,608,375,854,525
7	386,206,920	17	387,221,678,682,300
8	2,558,620,845	18	925,029,565,741,050
9	14,783,142,660	19	2,044,802,197,935,900
10	75,394,027,566	20	4,191,844,505,805,495

Figure 45. Amount of group combinations within 60 groups.

145

Combinations within 80			
1	80	11	10,477,677,064,400
2	3,160	12	60,246,643,120,300
3	82,160	13	315,136,287,090,800
4	1,581,580	14	1,508,152,231,077,400
5	24,040,016	15	6,635,869,816,740,560
6	300,500,200	16	26,958,221,130,508,525
7	3,176,716,400	17	101,489,773,667,796,800
8	28,987,537,150	18	355,214,207,837,288,800
9	231,900,297,200	19	1,159,120,046,626,942,400
10	1,646,492,110,120	20	3,535,316,142,212,174,320

Figure 46. Amount of group combinations within 80 groups.

Combinations within 40			
1	40	11	2,311,801,440
2	780	12	5,586,853,480
3	9,880	13	12,033,222,880
4	91,390	14	23,206,929,840
5	658,008	15	40,225,345,056
6	3,838,380	16	62,852,101,650
7	18,643,560	17	88,732,378,800
8	76,904,685	18	113,380,261,800
9	273,438,880	19	131,282,408,400
10	847,660,528	20	137,846,528,820

Figure 47. Amount of group combinations within 40 groups.

OUTCOMES FOR ALL TICKETS

When the total of the combinations of each ticket is played on one drawing, the number of tickets which produce each catch is shown. The total amount of tickets of each denomination is the number of combinations of each within 80, and these are shown in Figure 46.

1 Spot Ticket		2 Spot Ticket	
Tickets	Catch	Tickets	Catch
60	0	1,770	0
20	1	1,200	1
		190	2

Figure 48. Outcomes for all tickets.

146

3 Spot Ticket		4 Spot Ticket		5 Spot Ticket	
Tickets	Catch	Tickets	Catch	Tickets	Catch
34,220	0	487,635	0	5,461,512	0
35,400	1	684,400	1	9,752,700	1
11,400	2	336,300	2	6,501,800	2
1,140	3	68,400	3	2,017,800	3
		4,845	4	290,700	4
				15,504	5

6 Spot Ticket		7 Spot Ticket	
Tickets	Catch	Tickets	Catch
50,063,860	0	386,206,920	0
109,230,240	1	1,001,277,200	1
92,650,650	2	1,037,687,280	2
39,010,800	3	555,903,900	3
8,575,650	4	165,795,900	4
930,240	5	27,442,080	5
38,760	6	2,325,600	6
		77,520	7

8 Spot Ticket		9 Spot Ticket	
Tickets	Catch	Tickets	Catch
2,558,620,845	0	14,783,142,660	0
7,724,138,400	1	51,172,416,900	1
9,512,133,400	2	73,397,314,800	2
6,226,123,680	3	57,072,800,400	3
2,362,591,575	4	26,461,025,640	4
530,546,880	5	7,560,293,040	5
68,605,200	6	1,326,367,200	6
4,651,200	7	137,210,400	7
125,970	8	7,558,200	8
		167,960	9

Figure 48 (continued).

10 Spot Ticket		11 Spot Ticket	
Tickets	Catch	Tickets	Catch
75,394,027,566	0	342,700,125,300	0
295,662,853,200	1	1,507,880,551,320	1
486,137,960,550	2	2,808,797,105,400	2
440,275,888,800	3	2,916,827,763,300	3
242,559,401,700	4	1,871,172,527,400	4
84,675,282,048	5	776,190,085,440	5
18,900,732,600	6	211,688,205,120	6
2,652,734,400	7	37,801,465,200	7
222,966,900	8	4,310,693,400	8
10,077,600	9	297,289,200	9
184,756	10	11,085,360	10
		167,960	11

12 Spot Ticket		13 Spot Ticket	
Tickets	Catch	Tickets	Catch
1,399,358,844,975	0	5,166,863,427,600	0
6,854,002,506,000	1	27,987,176,899,500	1
14,324,865,237,540	2	65,113,023,807,000	2
16,852,782,632,400	3	85,949,191,425,240	3
12,396,517,994,025	4	71,624,326,187,700	4
5,987,752,087,680	5	39,668,857,580,880	5
1,940,475,213,600	6	14,969,380,219,200	6
423,376,410,240	7	3,880,950,427,200	7
61,427,380,950	8	687,986,666,640	8
5,747,591,200	9	81,903,174,600	9
327,018,120	10	6,322,350,320	10
10,077,600	11	297,289,200	11
125,970	12	7,558,200	12
		77,520	13

14 Spot Ticket		15 Spot Ticket	
Tickets	Catch	Tickets	Catch
17,345,898,649,800	0	53,194,089,192,720	0
103,337,268,552,000	1	346,917,972,996,000	1
265,878,180,545,250	2	981,704,051,244,000	2
390,678,142,842,000	3	1,595,269,083,271,500	3
365,284,063,557,270	4	1,660,382,107,078,500	4
229,197,843,800,640	5	1,168,909,003,383,264	5
99,172,143,952,200	6	572,994,609,501,600	6
29,938,760,438,400	7	198,344,287,904,400	7
6,306,544,444,200	8	48,650,485,712,400	8
917,315,555,520	9	8,408,725,925,600	9
90,093,492,060	10	1,009,047,111,072	10
5,747,591,200	11	81,903,174,600	11
222,966,900	12	4,310,693,400	12
4,651,200	13	137,210,400	13
38,760	14	2,325,600	14
		15,504	15

Figure 48 (continued).

High-Low 12 Spot Ticket

Tickets	Catch	Tickets	Catch
8,081,297,329,730,625	0–0–0	1,066,908,553,804,800	3–2–2
39,581,864,472,150,000	1–0–0	770,545,066,636,800	3–3–1
60,164,433,997,668,000	1–1–0	533,454,276,902,400	4–2–1
22,561,662,749,125,500	2–0–0	74,090,871,792,000	4–3–0
28,312,674,822,432,000	1–1–1	206,395,999,992,000	3–3–2
63,703,518,350,472,000	2–1–0	77,398,499,997,000	4–2–2
5,308,626,529,206,000	3–0–0	68,798,666,664,000	4–3–1
41,652,300,459,924,000	2–1–1	2,149,958,333,250	4–4–0
15,619,612,672,471,500	2–2–0	9,655,953,216,000	3–3–3
13,884,100,153,308,000	3–1–0	21,725,894,736,000	4–3–2
433,878,129,790,875	4–0–0	1,810,491,228,000	4–4–1
15,089,135,260,953,600	2–2–1	1,373,476,104,000	4–3–3
10,897,708,799,577,600	3–1–1	515,053,539,000	4–4–2
7,544,567,630,476,800	3–2–0	58,198,140,000	4–4–3
1.047,856,615,344,000	4–1–0	727,476,750	4–4–4
2,619,641,538,360,000	2–2–2		
6,985,710,768,960,000	3–2–1		
582,142,564,080,000	3–3–0	347,924,364,019,732,500	
582,142,564,080,000	4–1–1		
436,606,923,060,000	4–2–0		

High-Low 9 Spot Ticket

Tickets	Catch	Tickets	Catch
4,139,279,944,800	0–0–0	1,360,852,747,200	2–2–1
14,328,276,732,000	1–0–0	453,617,582,400	3–1–1
15,409,656,108,000	1–1–0	302,411,721,600	3–2–0
5,136,552,036,000	2–0–0	238,746,096,000	3–2–1
10,273,104,072,000	2–1–0	119,373,048,000	2–2–2
5,136,552,036,000	1–1–1	13,263,672,000	3–3–0
570,728,004,000	3–0–0	28,814,184,000	3–2–2
4,762,984,615,200	2–1–1	9,604,728,000	3–3–1
1,587,661,538,400	2–2–0	2,116,296,000	3–3–2
1,058,441,025,600	3–1–0	47,028,800	3–3–3
		64,932,083,216,000	

Figure 48 (continued).

The percentage of the gross wagers which is expected to be paid out on each ticket shown in the pay rate in figure

149

3, and also the percent represented by each winning catch, are shown in figure 49.

The figures shown for each catch are approximate, however the total percentages are accurate.

60-Cent 1 Spot Ticket		
Catch	Win	% Pay-Out
1	1.80	75%

60-Cent 2 Spot Ticket		
Catch	Win	% Pay-Out
2	$ 7.50	75.158%

60-Cent 3 Spot Ticket		
Catch	Win	% Pay-Out
2	$ .60	13.8
3	26.00	60
		74.002%

60-Cent 4 Spot Ticket		
Catch	Win	% Pay-Out
2	$ .60	21.3
3	2.50	18
4	70.00	35.7
		75.023%

60-Cent 5 Spot Ticket		
Catch	Win	% Pay-Out
3	$ .50	7
4	5.00	10
5	535.00	57.5
		74.507%

60-Cent 6 Spot Ticket		
Catch	Win	% Pay-Out
3	$ .35	7.5
4	2.00	9
5	60.00	31
6	1,250.00	26.9
		74.913%

60-Cent 7 Spot Ticket		
Catch	Win	% Pay-Out
4	$ .60	5.2
5	12.00	17.3
6	245.00	29.9
7	5,500.00	22.4
		74.758%

60-Cent 8 Spot Ticket		
Catch	Win	% Pay-Out
5	$ 5.00	15.2
6	50.00	19.7
7	1,100.00	29.4
8	12,500.00	9
		73.445%

40-Cent 9 Spot Ticket		
Catch	Win	% Pay-Out
4	$ .20	5.7
5	2.00	16.3
6	18.00	25.7
7	112.00	16.5
8	1,100.00	8.9
9	7,500.00	1.3
		74.632%

60-Cent 9 Spot Ticket		
Catch	Win	% Pay-Out
5	$ 2.00	10.8
6	30.00	28.5
7	175.00	17.1
8	3,000.00	16.7
9	12,500.00	1.5
		74.527%

Figure 49. Percentage probabilities of tickets shown on rate schedule in figure 3.

60-Cent 10 Spot Ticket		
Catch	Win	% Pay-Out
5	$ 1.20	10
6	12.00	23
7	90.00	24
8	660.00	14.9
9	2,400.00	2.4
10	12,000.00	.2
		74.980%

60-Cent 11 Spot Ticket		
Catch	Win	% Pay-Out
6	$ 6.00	20.2
7	50.00	30
8	250.00	17.1
9	1,200.00	5.6
10	7,500.00	1.3
11	12,500.00	.03
		74.442%

60-Cent 12 Spot Ticket		
Catch	Win	% Pay-Out
5	$ .50	8.3
6	3.00	16.2
7	18.00	21.1
8	130.00	22.2
9	375.00	6
10	900.00	.8
11	5,000.00	.1
12	25,000.00	.01
		74.485%

60-Cent 13 Spot Ticket		
Catch	Win	% Pay-Out
6	$ 1.00	7.9
7	10.00	20.5
8	50.00	18.2
9	450.00	19.5
10	2,400.00	8
11	4,500.00	.7
12	10,000.00	.04
13	25,000.00	.001
		74.874%

60-Cent 14 Spot Ticket		
Catch	Win	% Pay-Out
6	$ 2.00	21.9
7	5.00	16.6
8	20.00	14
9	160.00	16.3
10	500.00	5
11	1,500.00	.9
12	5,000.00	.1
13	15,000.00	.007
14	25,000.00	.0001
		74.685%

60-Cent 15 Spot Ticket		
Catch	Win	% Pay-Out
6	$ 1.00	14.4
7	5.00	24.9
8	14.00	17.1
9	50.00	10.5
10	150.00	3.8
11	1,500.00	3.1
12	5,000.00	.5
13	15,000.00	.05
14	20,000.00	.001
15	25,000.00	.00001
		74.447%

Figure 49 (continued).

The pay rate shown on page 10, which was used on the games in Philadelphia before the turn of the century, produced an expected gross profit of 25.4 percent, which is about the same as the pay rates in figure 3.

The win schedule for the early Chinese games described on page 7 had an expected profit of 33.4 percent. Their money values have changed often during the past several hundred years and these values were not necessarily the same between different areas. The value of a tael of silver, the "ounce" of China, often varied with the market price and the finenes of the silver, and was sometimes worth from 700 to 2,000 cash. "Cash" was the name of their smallest valued coin and was equal in value to the term "li." Tael is a unit of weight and one tael is equal in value to 10 mace, 100 candareens, 1,000 cash. However, this figure of 33.4 percent represents generally the expected profit.

The different rates of pay used in this game throughout the years have produced expected gross profits ranging from less than 20 percent to more than 40 percent but have mostly averaged from 25 to 30 percent.

40 Spot Wager

In 1967 the Pioneer Club of Las Vegas considered offering a wager that had not been seen for several years. This was a bet that more than half (eleven or more) of the winning numbers would appear in one-half of the ticket, either the upper or lower half; a player could bet on either half. The winning odds would be 6 to 5 (a $5.00 winning bet would receive $11.00). This bet was not offered but a similar bet was in play for a short time at the Dunes Hotel. It had very few takers and was soon discontinued.

Keno wagers have differed from time to time throughout Nevada but this difference is mostly in the rates for winning pays. However, the pay rates are usually standard within local areas.

The probabilities of this proposed wager is the same as that of any selected forty numbers, and is figured on the basis of a 40 spot ticket, just as the other ticket probabilities are figured. The outcome for the 40 spot ticket is depicted:

Amount of Tickets	Catch	Amount of Tickets	Catch
137,846,528,820	0	632,136,396,535,987,200	11
5,251,296,336,000	1	429,655,207,020,553,800	12
88,436,604,204,000	2	224,342,112,756,652,800	13
876,675,902,544,000	3	89,077,015,359,259,200	14
5,744,053,569,793,500	4	26,468,598,849,608,448	15
26,468,598,849,608,448	5	5,744,053,569,793,500	16
89,077,015,359,259,200	6	876,675,902,544,000	17
224,342,112,756,652,800	7	88,436,604,204,000	18
429,655,207,020,553,800	8	5,251,296,336,000	19
632,136,396,535,987,200	9	137,846,528,820	20
718,528,370,729,238,784	10	3,535,316,142,212,174,320	

Outcome for 40 spot ticket.

If $5.00 is wagered on each of these tickets and $11.00 is paid out on each of the 1,408,393,885,741,467,768 tickets which catch eleven or more spots, then 88 percent of the amount wagered is paid out in wins.

From the above results it can be determined how often a given amount of drawn numbers is expected to appear within any forty numbers. Until about 1960 it was common on many games to occasionally announce the amount of drawn numbers which were in the upper and the lower halves of the ticket, such as "it's a twelve and eight draw," meaning that twelve of the drawn numbers are in the upper half of the ticket and eight numbers are in the lower half.

Draw		Expected Frequency	Draw		Expected Frequency	
10 & 10	once each	2.5 draws	16 & 4	"	2	days
11 & 9	"	2.8 "	17 & 3	"	13	"
12 & 8	"	4.1 "	18 & 2	"	4½	months
13 & 7	"	7.3 "	19 & 1	"	6	years
14 & 6	"	20 "	20 & 0	"	238	"
15 & 5	"	68 "				

Some expected frequencies.

Draws of ten and ten through fourteen and six occur very frequently, and the only such draws that are rare are a twenty and ought as well as a nineteen and one. The expected frequency of these such draws are shown above, without regard to which ticket half the amounts of numbers may appear. The frequencies expressed in time are figured on a basis of 150 draws per day.

A draw of 19 and one has been seen by many who have worked on the game a few years, but a draw of 20 and 0 has been witnessed by very few. However, with the number of games operating in Nevada, a 20 and 0 draw should have occurred several times.

The probabilities of this 40 spot ticket was used to design a couple of wagers offered on a few games today. These tickets are known as "TOP AND BOTTOM" and as "CALL SHOT TOP OR BOTTOM." The pay rate for the CALL SHOT TOP OR BOTTOM is shown below.

CALL SHOT TOP OR BOTTOM BET $1.00 OR ANY AMOUNT			
Call 10 & 10 Pays...$ 3.50		Call 15 & 5 Pays...$ 90.00	
Call 11 & 9 Pays...$ 4.00		Call 5 & 15 Pays...$ 90.00	
Call 9 & 11 Pays...$ 4.00		Call ANY 15 & 5 Pays...$ 45.00	
Call ANY 11 & 9 Pays...$ 2.00		Call 16 & 4 Pays...$ 450.00	
Call 12 & 8 Pays...$ 6.00		Call 4 & 16 Pays...$ 450.00	
Call 8 & 12 Pays...$ 6.00		Call ANY 16 & 4 Pays...$ 225.00	
Call ANY 12 & 8 Pays...$ 3.00		Call 17 & 3 Pays...$ 3,000.00	
Call 13 & 7 Pays...$ 11.00		Call 3 & 17 Pays...$ 3,000.00	
Call 7 & 13 Pays...$ 11.00		Call ANY 17 & 3 Pays...$ 1,500.00	
Call ANY 13 & 7 Pays...$ 5.50		Call 18 & 2 Pays...$25,000.00	
Call 14 & 6 Pays...$ 30.00		Call 2 & 18 Pays...$25,000.00	
Call 6 & 14 Pays...$ 30.00		Call ANY 18 & 2 Pays...$12,500.00	
Call ANY 14 & 6 Pays...$ 15.00		Call ANY 19 & 1 Pays...$25,000.00	
—OR— Call ANY 20 & 0 Pays...$25,000.00			

Call shot pay rate.

For the TOP AND BOTTOM wager it makes no difference which half (top or bottom) of the ticket contains which amount of catch to win. A draw of 5 and 15 or a draw of 15 and 5 pays the same. Shown below is the pay rate for a $2.00 TOP AND BOTTOM ticket.

A TOP AND BOTTOM ticket is played by writing the amount of the wager in the margin and in the body of the

154

ticket write a "T" in the upper half and a "B" in the lower half.

$2.00 TOP AND BOTTOM TICKET				
Catch	Win		Catch	Win
13 – 7	$	2.00	17 – 3	$ 400.00
14 – 6		6.00	18 – 2	2,000.00
15 – 5		20.00	19 – 1	10,000.00
16 – 4		80.00	20 – 0	25,000.00

Top & bottom pay rate.

These tickets are not known very well yet and only time will tell if they "catch on."

A wager could also be designed for betting on twenty selected numbers, and the outcome for a 20 spot ticket is shown below.

Amount of Tickets	Catch	Amount of Tickets	Catch
4,191,844,505,805,495	0	2,482,976,641,173,600	11
40,896,043,959,078,000	1	322,309,467,844,650	12
175,755,617,490,799,500	2	29,938,760,438,400	13
441,432,713,697,822,000	3	1,940,475,213,600	14
724,852,581,015,173,625	4	84,675,282,048	15
824,721,158,843,930,880	5	2,362,591,575	16
672,327,031,666,248,000	6	39,010,800	17
400,535,252,907,552,000	7	336,300	18
176,277,233,701,500,750	8	1,200	19
57,559,913,045,388,000	9	1	20
13,929,498,956,983,396	10	3,535,316,142,212,174,320	

Outcome for 20 spot ticket.

This outcome reflects the expected results of any twenty selected numbers, and, as 20 numbers are drawn each game, it can be determined from this outcome how often a given amount of those numbers that were drawn on one game is expected to repeat as winning numbers on the next game. Shown below is the expected frequency of each. The frequencies expressed in time are figured on the basis of 150 draws per day.

155

Amount of Repeat Numbers	Frequency of Occurrence		
5	Once each	4.2	draws
4	"	4.8	"
6	"	5	"
3	"	8	"
7	"	9	"
8	"	20	"
2	"	20	"
9	"	62	"
1	"	88	"
10	"	252	"
0	"	6	days
11	"	10	"
12	"	73	"
13	"	26	months
14	"	33	years
15	"	779	"
16	"	27,777	"
17	"	1,670,000	"
18	"	195,000,000	"
19	"	54,550,000,000	"
20	"	64,000,000,000,000	"

Expected frequency of repeat numbers.

Thirteen repeat numbers in two consecutive draws have occurred many times, and it's believed that fourteen repeat numbers have been seen; but it seems that no one has ever heard of a greater amount.

Sometimes the spots played on a ticket consist only of numbers that were drawn on the previous game, especially when the trend seems to lean this way: that is when a greater than usual amount of the winning numbers from one drawing continue to repeat as winning numbers on the next drawing. (Many players will detect such a trend, as the results of each drawing are carefully observed.) These numbers have as good a chance of being drawn on the next game, or on any game, as any other numbers, because each drawing is a process independent of any other. But there are times when the numbers seem to (and do) repeat more than usual and sometimes this trend will continue for several drawings.

We have shown the expected frequency of the occurrence of each amount of repeat winning numbers: now let's examine the expected number of times that each amount of repeat numbers should occur within 1000 draws, along with an actual such count of 1000 continuous games.

Amount of Repeat Numbers	Mathematical Expectancy	Actual Count
0	1	1
1	11	3
2	49	54
3	123	125
4	205	188
5	235	253
6	197	179
7	110	119
8	49	56
9	16	17
10	4	5
11	0	0
	1000	1000

Mathematical frequency and actual count . . .

This actual count is not consistent with the mathematical average, and is not expected to be, however, this count would become closer to the expected average as more draws are compared and counted, but would never necessarily be exact.

The outcome of the 20 spot ticket indicates that two identical draws are expected to occur consecutively, on any one game, once each 64,000,000,000,000 years. This

157

probability considers only the twenty winning numbers and not the sequence in which they may be drawn. There are 2,432,902,008,176,640,000 permutations of twenty objects (sequences in which they may be arranged), and so the probability of the occurrence of two consecutive identical draws in the same sequence is once each 150,000,000,000,000,000,000,000,000,000,000,000 years. On some games the balls of each drawing are photographed, and this indicates the likeliness of the occurrence of two consecutive identical photographs.

There are many probabilities of this game that serve no useful function except as a matter of interest. One such ratio is the expected length of time that a given ticket will be played before all of the spots are caught. Figure 27 shows the probability of each catch for all tickets, and these results for the 8 spot ticket are shown below.

AVERAGE NUMBER OF 8 SPOT TICKETS PLAYED FOR EACH OF THE CORRESPONDING CATCHES	
Tickets	Catch
230,114.6	8
6,232.2	7
422.5	6
54.6	5
12.2	4
4.6	3
3.0	2
3.7	1
11.3	0

Probability of the 8 spot.

The average number of tickets played before one of them catches all 8 spots (230,115) indicates that if an 8 spot ticket is played on every game drawn for eight hours each day, it is expected to catch all 8 spots once each thirteen years. This does not mean that it would occur within that time, or that it would ever occur, but only that it is expected. It could also happen much sooner. All the spots were caught once on the first 8 spot ticket the player had ever played.

The odds against catching all 8 spots does not indicate the player's true chances because of the other winning catches. Only nine percent of the total amount wagered is paid out for a catch of all 8 spots. For each ticket that catches all 8 spots, shown below is the number of tickets that is expected to produce each of the other catches.

Tickets	Catch
1	8
37	7
544	6
4,211	5
18,755	4
49,425	3
75,511	2
61,317	1
20,311	0

For each 8 spot ticket that catches all 8 spots, these amounts of tickets will catch the other amounts of spots.

The amount of money paid out for a catch of 8 spots on the 8 spot ticket is very small as compared to the amounts paid out for the other winning catches.

When all the probabilities are analyzed it can be realized that the best ticket to play is a matter of personal choice. It can also be realized that the operation of this game is a business; like that of many other types. The percentage odds with the house is comparable to a broker's fee in some types of business; and to show a profit, the game must operate efficiently.

CHAPTER

Wagering Rules

The spots on a ticket may be arranged by different methods of grouping so as to produce different amounts of ways, and these amounts can vary from just a few up to many in meeting the player's desire. Shown below is a ticket with the spots divided into groups of 4 in each, and each 4 spot group is further divided into 2 spot groups.

Figure 50. A 3 way 8 spot marked with 6-2s.

The 4 spot groups on this ticket are not being played, as such, and the only reason for these groups is to limit the amount of 8 spot ways to three. If this ticket was marked with only groups of 2 spots in each, there would be fifteen 8 spot ways ($C \frac{6}{4} = 15$), and if each spot was kinged, making each spot a group of one, there would be 495 combinations of 8 spots ($C \frac{12}{8} = 495$).

161

This ticket could also be played, as marked, as a 12 way 6 spot. These 12 ways are made up by combining each 4 spot group with each of the other 2 spot groups. These spots could also be grouped as shown below to make up other amounts of ways.

Figure 51. A 7 way 8 spot marked with 6-2s.

The grouping on this ticket now makes up 7 combinations of 8 spots and 8 combinations of 6 spots. Other amounts of spots could also be played, and other methods of grouping, which there are many, could make up many other amounts of ways.

The ticket shown in Figure 52 is similar in structure, with the spots divided into 4 groups of 6 spots, and each 6 spot group is further divided into groups of 2 spots in each.

The 6 spot wagers consist of each of the 6 spot groups. The 4 spot ways are made up of two 2 spot groups within each 6 spot group (the 4 spot combinations within each 6 spot group, which makes 3 ways within each) making a total of twelve 4 spot ways. The customary method of conditioning this wager on the 4 spot ways is shown on the ticket and indicates four different 3 way 4 spot wagers, which makes a total twelve. This type of conditioning often makes a ticket easier to read than if it was conditioned as a 12 way 4 spot.

Figure 52. An unusual multiple way ticket.

Each of the 10 spot ways is made up from all the spots in one of the 6 spot groups combined with a 4 spot arrangement within one of the other 6 spot groups. Three such 4 spot combinations within each of the remaining 6 spot groups make 9 ways of combining 4 spots with each 6 spot group to make up 10 spots, and a total of 36 ways from this arrangement ($C\frac{3}{3}$ x $C\frac{3}{2}$ x 3 x 4 = 36).

This ticket is played only on rare occasions, and is usually played for only the 10 spot ways as shown. However, there are other arrangements of 10 spots that could be played. One such other arrangement is two 2 spot groups within one 6 spot group combined with the same in another 6 spot group plus one 2 spot group from either of the remaining 6 spot groups. This arrangement makes up 324 combinations of 10 spots ($C\frac{3}{2}$ x $C\frac{3}{2}$ x $C\frac{6}{1}$ x 6 = 324).

Another arrangement consists of two 2 spot groups within one of the 6 spot groups combined with one 2 spot

163

group from each of the other 6 spot groups, which makes up another 324 combinations of 10 spots ($C\frac{3}{2}$x $C\frac{3}{1}$x $C\frac{3}{1}$x $C\frac{3}{1}$x 4 = 324).

The arrangement of all the spots in one 6 spot group plus one 2 spot group from each of two other 6 spot groups make up 108 combinations of 10 spots ($C\frac{3}{3}$x $C\frac{3}{1}$x $C\frac{3}{1}$x 3 x 4 = 108).

If the spots on this ticket were marked only in groups of two in each (not further divided into 6 spot groups) there would be only one arrangement of 10 spot ways. This one arrangement produces 792 combinations ($C\frac{12}{5}$ = 792), and this amount is the same as the total of all the above arrangements.

The ways of other even-numbered amounts of spots on this ticket could also be played, and by changing one of the 2 spot groups into two separate one spot groups, or by just kinging the spots within one of these groups, the arrangements of odd-numbered amounts of spots could also be played.

Figure 53. A deuce way 8 spot marked with kings so that the 9s can also be played.

Shown in figure 53 is a type of ticket that is often marked for the purpose of playing the even and the odd numbered amounts of spots.

The spots that are kinged on the above ticket are eliminated, one at a time, while the others are counted to make up the four combinations of 9 spots. And by eliminating each of the 2 spot groups, one at a time, the five combinations of 8 spots are formed. If the kings were not further grouped into 2 spot groups, there would be nine combinations of 8 spots. This ticket could also be played for the ways of all the even and odd numbered amounts of spots up to ten.

The next illustration shows a ticket with all of the spots kinged and further divided into two equal groups; a method in which this ticket is sometimes played.

Figure 54. An unusual 70 way 10 spot ticket.

The seventy combinations of 10 spots on this ticket are made up from the arrangement of all the spots in the first 7 spot group plus the 3 spot combinations of the second 7 spot group, then (the same arrangement) all the

165

spots in the second 7 spot group plus the 3 spot combinations of the first 7 spot group ($C\frac{7}{7}$x $C\frac{7}{3}$x 2 = 70).

Like the illustration in figure 86, there are also other 10 spot arrangements on this ticket; the total combinations of which are equal to the total of such ways within fourteen kings.

The arrangement of 6 spots from one 7 spot group and 4 spots from the other 7 spot group make up a 490 way 10 spot ($C\frac{7}{6}$x $C\frac{7}{4}$x 2 = 490). And the 5 spot combinations within each 7 spot group are combined to make a 441 way 10 spot ($C\frac{7}{5}$x $C\frac{7}{5}$ = 441).

If these kings were not divided (no line drawn across the ticket) there would be only one arrangement of 10 spots; ten kings. This one arrangement would create 1,001 ways ($C\frac{14}{10}$ = 1,001), and this amount is the same as the total of all the above combinations.

Any one, or any combination of these arrangements may be played, and by cutting the ticket differently (6 and 8, or 5 and 9, etc.) other amounts of ways may be created.

Shown in figure 55 is another ticket that is constructed in an unusual manner. This ticket, like the one in figure 54, was played only on rare occasions.

The 9 spot ways that are invariably played on this ticket are made up of the arrangements of two 4 spot groups and the single king, which makes 3 ways; and the 3 groups of 3 spots, which makes the fourth 9 spot way.

The High-Low wager consists of the 3 groups of 4 spots.

The 10 spot ways that are being played are made up of arrangements of two 3 spot groups and one 4 spot group, which makes 9 ways; the 3 groups of 3 spots and the single king make up one 10 spot way; and the 3 groups of 3 spots plus each of the group kings, one at a time, make 12 ways, for a total of 22 ways.

166

Figure 55. This complex way ticket was occasionally played several years ago. Such a ticket is good for teaching student Keno writers.

This ticket is so constructed that there are many arrangements of ways other than those being played. Nine High-Low ways may be made up of two 4 spot groups with one 3 spot group and the single king. The arrangement of two 4 spot groups with the single king and one group king from the other 4 spot group makes a 12 way 10 spot. (The number of ways in this arrangement coincides with that of another arrangement mentioned above.) One 3 spot group combined with the 7 spot combinations of the group kings make up a 5,184 way 10 spot. Other arrangements make up thousands of other 10 spot ways. And thousands of 9 spot ways may also be made up of different arrangements.

Some of the wagers discussed on the aforementioned tickets may be considered undesirable and may not be accepted on all games. Any wager, when the terms are clearly understood and agreed upon by the parties involved, may under certain conditions be considered valid. But Keno wagers are made with one party and a win may be collected from any of several others; therefore, when a proposed wager gets beyond a given

167

point of complexity it may not be accepted by many game managers. However, some undesirable tickets are accepted, if they are valid, when the amount of the wager is sufficient to justify its acceptance.

High-Low wagers are generally accepted only when the ticket is marked with groups of 4 spots in each. Shown here is a differently marked valid 3 way High-Low ticket. This particular ticket is considered undesirable and is generally not accepted.

Figure 56. An undesirable 3 way High-Low ticket.

There are just 12 spots on this ticket, so each high-low way makes use of all the spots. And these 3 ways are the number of ways that the four different 2 spot groups can be circled into two separate 4 spot groups. It would seem that there is no particular reason for playing a ticket such as this as the amount of spots caught would be the same number for each way. There will be a possible difference in the amount of spots caught within each 4 spot group, but the difference in the amounts won from each way, as compared to a single wager of the same amount (a wager on just one high-low way), would be insufficient to justify such a ticket.

168

Invalid Tickets

There are several methods in which invalid way tickets have been marked, and some of them have been played. Shown below is a High-Low way ticket that is invalid.

Figure 57. An invalid 4 way High-Low ticket.

This ticket would be valid when played as a 4 way 4 spot; and because 4 groups of 4 spots make a 4 way high-low, this ticket was accepted on a few games many years ago as a valid wager. Wins were paid on the basis of counting the king with each 3 spot group, thinking that the effect was the same as 4 groups of 4 spots; not realizing that such a wager changed the odds to favor the player because only 10 spots are used for each way.

This ticket was played quite regular by one individual over a period of many months, on a few games that would accept it, with only a small amount of success in winning. This is not unusual, even though the odds were in his favor, as it's normal for the outcome of any event of chance to require a long run to attain an expected average, and this required length of time for Keno wagers is much longer than for most gambling events.

On one occasion, when this ticket was winning small amounts, the player continued to change the ticket each few games by adding more ways. Groups of 3 spots were added, and then more kings were added until 100 ways were reached as shown below.

Figure 58. An invalid 100 way High-Low ticket.

This ticket could be considered a valid 1200 way high-low wager by combining the combinations of three 3 spot groups with three kings as an arrangement (one king with each 3 spot group) to make three 4 spot groups (C_3^6 x C_3^5 x 6 = 1200). (Three kings can be arranged six different ways with three 3 spot groups.) This ticket wager was accepted; however, it was on the same basis of the first ticket, which makes up 100 ways.

Within a few games while this ticket was being played, a draw came out that produced a large win. Four of the kings were caught, all the spots within two 3 spot groups were caught and one spot was caught in each of two other 3 spot groups. A great amount of confusion followed in trying to determine the amount of the win; after an hour or more had passed, the ticket was declared erroneous, and the amount wagered on that draw was

170

refunded. Such a ticket as this was no longer accepted on that game, and within minutes the other games that had previously accepted this ticket had learned of this incident, after which no one accepted the wager.

During the time this ticket (the one shown in figure 57) was being played it was accepted on one game, even though it was known to be invalid, only because the action was desirable. Then the ball bearing the number that was marked as the king was held out and never drawn as a winning number.

The validity of any way ticket may be tested by marking each of the ways on a separate ticket. If this is done for the two tickets that are shown above it will be seen that a high-low wager does not exist.

Figure 59. An invalid 3 way 8 spot. It contains only two 8 spots.

The above was accepted on a few games many years ago, and, like the two previous tickets, it is also invalid as it's played. The manner of grouping these upper groups is not customary and in essence the ticket contains one 4 spot group, two 3 spot groups and one king.

171

An attempt to mark each of these ways on a separate ticket will show that only two 8 spot ways exist.

The circling of spots to include them in more than one group can make up a valid ticket but such is considered undesirable and is usually not permitted, and for good reason. It is not necessary and it adds nothing to the game. Two such tickets are illustrated in figures 60 and 61.

The tail drawn from the spot on number 53 in figure 61 means that number is not being played. This is the method used by the writers to "take off a spot" that was marked in error. This practice is limited to the inside tickets.

Figure 60. An undesirable way ticket.

Occasionally, a ticket like that shown in figure 62 is presented for play and invariably the player wishes to wager on the 8 spot ways that are made up by combining the field (the uncircled group) with each of the other groups. This is a valid ticket wager but the manner in which it's marked makes it undesirable on some games; a few games will not accept such a ticket.

172

Figure 61. Another undesirable method of grouping spots. The spot on number 53 has been "taken off" and is not in play.

Figure 62 & 63. These tickets are marked in an unusual manner but both are valid wagers.

Some games will require the field group to be divided into two 2 spot groups and the ticket be conditioned 4-2-2.

173

And some games will require the ticket to be remarked as in figure 63.

Figure 63. A valid wager.

A similarly-marked ticket that was once very popular with the Chinese was marked with 16 groups of 5 spots in each and played as a 15 way 10 spot. Spots were actually marked on the numbers of only one of these groups, to distinguish this group from the others, and this group was used with each of the others to make the 15 ways. The numbers in each of the 15 groups that were not spotted were so arranged that they could be separated from all other numbers with a line.

Erroneous Tickets

Many tickets are played which contain errors in varying degrees. Most of these errors are of a minor nature and do not constitute an invalid wager. A common error is a ticket marked with an amount of spots that differ from the conditioning figure written in the margin. This is not considered an invalid wager, unless there are sixteen or more spots marked, *because a win is paid according to the amount of spots on the ticket rather than by the figure written in the margin.* Should the ticket be condi-

174

tioned an 8 spot but have 9 spots marked on it, *a win would be paid on the basis of a 9 spot ticket.*

A mismarked ticket is not considered an error because the payment of a win is made from the original ticket. *The purpose for making a duplicate copy of each ticket is primarily to provide the player with a receipt which will identify the owner of each wager in the event of a win.* It also provides the player a copy which he may compare with the drawing results and which may be replayed on another game. When this duplicate copy is replayed it then becomes the original ticket (of another duplicate copy) and the wager of record, and should it have been mismarked the wager is changed accordingly (provided the error is not caught).

Mismarked tickets occasionally cause some dissatisfaction among players that are not aware of this rule. But actually a mismarked ticket causes no loss to a player because the wager is recorded as submitted by the player, and when a mismarked ticket is replayed without correcting the mistake, it's either the player's error or intention. Many mismarked tickets are intentionally replayed without correcting the mistake. Sometimes an experienced player will do this so that he might complain and try to collect if the old numbers should produce a win several games later. In an attempt to bring this rule to the attention of players, it is stated in some rate books: *"Make sure your ticket is marked correctly, because the copy you hold is merely a receipt."*

Until recently there was an exception to this rule on the few games that use the carbon copy method of writing tickets. Until the rule was changed, these games used the duplicate copy as the wager of record. For a time during the latter part of the nineteenth century, some of the Chinese games in America used the duplicate copy as the recorded wager; but this was not satisfactory to the players, and since about 1900 all Chinese games in this country have used the original ticket as the wager of record.

Some players think of the original ticket only as the first ticket played regardless of how many times the duplicate copies may have been replayed, not realizing that *each copy when replayed becomes the original of another duplicate.* Some games use the term "inside ticket" rather than original ticket, which may be more clearly understood by some players.

Should a writer ever, by mistake or otherwise, give the original ticket to the player and retain the duplicate, then the duplicate copy (inside ticket) becomes the wager of record.

Game of Many Wagers

There are so many different ways of making a Keno wager that it would seemingly run into infinity. Sometimes tickets are presented for play that require much time to determine validity, and on some games all tickets presented are accepted and written, except when an error is obvious; should a ticket later be determined erroneous, the wager is refunded. For this reason a rule is printed on most tickets that reads: "Tickets with errors not corrected before game are void." Such a rule

Figure 64. An erroneous ticket.

176

means that the *wager is not binding, even though the money was accepted, if the ticket should be erroneous.*

In determining the validity of a ticket, only the wager as recorded is considered. The *intent* of the wager, except in extreme cases, *is never a supporting factor.*

When playing a ticket it is much better to play for the purpose of winning rather than marking a complicated ticket to test the mathematical ability of the writer.

The wager on the ticket in figure 64 is in error as there are four different combinations of 12 spots and nothing to indicate which is being wagered on. A line drawn across the ticket separating one group from the others would make this a valid wager. It may have been so marked intentionally in the hope that a win might be collected and that the number of spots might be overlooked.

A win on this ticket could be figured and prorated in several ways. The 4 spot wins could be figured at a 25¢ wager on each and the 12 spot wins as a 12½¢ wager on each, or each of these wins could be figured at the minimum wager which, at the rates in figure 3, would equal a $3.00 ticket (25¢ on each 4 spot and 50¢ on each 12 spot way) and this total win prorated to the $1.50 wager, or one-half. Each of these methods would produce different results and an average of these amounts could be paid, or the 12 spot wager could be refunded and wins paid on the 4 spot wagers.

When tickets contain wagers with an element of uncertainty, such as this one, they are usually declared erroneous.

Misspotted Ticket

Shown in figure 65 is a facsimile of an original ticket that was actually played. When a ticket like this is presented the writer determines from the player which numbers should be marked and writes the ticket accordingly, changing the inside copy to match. Without changing the inside copy such a ticket creates an element of uncertainty sufficient to be declared erroneous. Not all such tickets are declared erroneous and if a player's intent can be determined a win is paid accordingly. (Should such a ticket have been played on one or more games before the error is noticed, then that first copy is no longer considered the wager of record as it would no longer be the inside ticket.)

Figure 65. A misspotted ticket.

In marking a ticket with a brush it is essential that the spots are marked in a manner to clearly indicate the numbers being played, and when marked with crayon each number should be marked with an "X."

Prorating

Tickets are often played with a wager amount other than the base rate or a multiple thereof, especially way tickets. These are never considered erroneous because of a wrong price, and these wins are prorated and paid accordingly. Should the ticket have more than one rate of pay and not be conditioned to show which rate was played, then the rate selected for payment is at the discretion of the club.

178

Prorating is a convenient method of determining the correct win, which is a ratio of an amount that would have been won at the correct wager price, and is equal to the ratio difference of the actual wager and the correct wager. On way tickets it is sometimes more convenient to use a ratio consisting of the number of ways involved, when this ratio is the same as that of the difference in the wagers, because a ratio of the amount of ways is always in even numbers. We show a ticket from which the win can be easily prorated to a ratio of the number of ways involved.

Figure 66. A missconditioned ticket, but still a valid wager.

At 55¢ per way the price of this ticket is correct for the "conditioned 35 ways;" however, there are only 20 ways on the ticket. The addition of one more group of 3 spots would make 35 ways, and the omission of such a group is a common error. (A more common error is a ticket containing too many groups.) The actual wager per way is 96¼¢, and the total ticket win at 55¢ per way could be prorated to this amount which is a fractional ratio of $\frac{96¼}{55}$. Or this 55¢ win could be prorated at the ratio of the ticket wagers which is $\frac{19.25}{11}$. (Eleven dollars is the cor-

179

rect wager at 55¢ per way.) Each of these price differences are the same ratio, and both are uneven numbers. The difference of the ways involved is also the same ratio, and because these are already even numbers, it is more convenient to prorate to this figure: $\frac{35}{20}$ which may quickly be reduced to $\frac{7}{4}$. At 55¢ per way, a catch of 3-2-1-1-0-0 would win $60.00, according to the rate schedule in figure 10, and this amount multiplied by $\frac{7}{4}$ prorates the win to $105.00. When there are more ways on the ticket than are paid for, the win is prorated to a lesser amount accordingly.

All prorating involves ratios; and when a ratio can be used that is already an even-numbered fraction or percentage, the problem is more easily solved.

Prorating The Limit

The limit on most games of chance is applied to the wager amount, which is convenient when there are only two possible outcomes: lose or win one given amount. This type of limit would not be practical for a Keno game because most Keno wagers have several different possible outcomes, each winning outcome producing a different amount. Because of this, and the tremendously high payoffs that can be won on this game, it is necessary that a limit be set to establish casino liabilities rather than setting a limit on the amount wagered. Most Nevada casinos have set the limit of their liabilities at $25,000 *for each Keno drawing*.

Many players today think the amount of the game limit applies to each winning ticket, not realizing that this amount is a liability limit for the total of all wins on each drawing, even though it is stated in all rate books that the limit is the "total payout for each drawing," or "limit each game to aggregate players," or some other similar wording.

The Chinese players of San Francisco were well aware of how the limit was applied, and these Chinese games had frequent occasions for prorating the limit. These games operated with different limits, ranging from about

$1,000 up to $30,000. This limit on some of the games represented the company's entire capital; and when the wins on one drawing totaled more than the limit, all wins were prorated. Companies that had more capital than their limit often prorated wins as small as $17.80 simply because they were not liable for a greater amount.

The limit of liability did not establish a limit that a ticket could win, but an amount that would satisfy all losses. So in prorating this limit, each winning ticket was paid off at the same ratio, proportional to the ticket win. The amount each ticket had won was thought of as shares, and the total of all wins represented the amount of shares involved. The ratio of the limit to the total amount of all wins established a rate (ratio) by which all winning shares were paid. If a drawing on a $3,000 limit game produced a win of $3,600 on one ticket, and other wins which totaled another $400 ($4,000 in total wins), then all winning tickets were paid off at seventy-five percent of their face value.

There have been very few occasios on the Caucasian games to prorate a limit payout, and on the few such known occasions there have been only two or three large wins involved, none of which had won an amount greater than the limit. All other wins, some up to several hundred dollars, were paid in full, intentionally making the total amount paid out considerably more than the limit of liability. This is the custom today, and *up to about $30,000 is occasionally paid* on one drawing without prorating the wins.

The limit on the games today serves the same purpose as it always has — to limit the club's liabilities for losses on each drawing. All rate schedules show an amount not greater than the limit, as a maximum that any ticket will win, and in a sense this is correct as no more than this amount can be collected. However, there is actually no limit on the amount a ticket can win, and in a case when the limit is prorated the actual win on each ticket determines the amount of shares that each winner will receive.

181

When a ticket that is played on two games, like the double action tickets mentioned on page 76, is involved in a draw where the limit is prorated, *only the portion of win resulting from that draw is prorated.* Any amount of win produced by the other draw would be paid in full.

CHAPTER

Playing Methods

Players use many methods in selecting numbers to play. A few players spot their numbers at random, without any particular choice of selection, but most tickets are marked with specific numbers. The specific numbers selected may be certain numbers which the player is associated with, such as a telephone number, a street address, ages, social security number, etc., or they may be numbers selected because of their location on the ticket. Many players closely observe each drawing and, from these results, try their luck at guessing the next game's winning numbers; these are usually selected only for their location on the ticket. The Chinese people often mark numbers for their corresponding word meaning from their old poem, which is translated herein.

Some players seldom change their numbers, continuing to play the same ones each game, while others continually mark new tickets, changing their numbers each game or every few games. Playing the same numbers each game is referred to as *"waiting."* This alludes to the soldiers in the mountains in search of the monkeys, each soldier waiting for the monkeys to come to his mountain. Changing the numbers each game is referred to as *"chasing"* and relates to the *soldiers moving from mountain to mountain in search of the monkeys.* Very large amounts have been won with either method, and they both can be equally effective.

A method used by many players to select numbers is to observe the results of several drawings and try to detect a behavior pattern of the balls. Sometimes the winning numbers will appear to be scattered haphazardly over the whole flashboard and may continue in this fashion over a period of several games. (Draws of this type seldom produce a large win.) Then at times the winning numbers will seem to appear in clusters for several games and may seem to persist within a certain area of the flashboard. Or the concentration of these winning numbers may seem to move rhythmically between certain locations on the flashboard.

These patterns may be quite obvious *after* they occur, but the challenge is to predict which will be the winning numbers *before they occur*.

Amount of Spots To Play

The trend over the past several years indicates that most players prefer to play tickets with longer odds. This is evidenced by the fact that the 8 spot is the most popular of all tickets played today, and while it contains the fewest number of spots that can win $25,000 for a $1 wager, it is also the least likely of all the tickets to produce a win of any size. Only one 8 spot ticket out of each 48 played will produce a win, while the 4 spot will produce one win out of each 3.8 tickets played. The probability of a win on all other tickets falls between these two figures. (See figure 28.)

Because the 8 spot is the most popular ticket played, more limit wins are paid on this ticket than on any other. Five wins of $25,000 were paid by one casino within a period of twelve days, all on 8 spot tickets. Tickets with fewer than 8 spots could win the limit more often because as fewer spots are played the chances of catching all of them increase; also, the winning odds decrease in proportion because the amount of the win for each catch is more or less in proportion to its probability. So, as fewer spots are played, a larger wager is required to win the limit. And, when the wager is sufficient, the limit may be won on most tickets with a catch of less than all the spots.

By playing 12 or more spots a win of $25,000 is possible with a minimum wager of 70¢, however this requires a catch of all the spots and such a catch is not very likely. The odds against catching all the spots on a 12 spot ticket are 478,261,832 to one, and such a catch has been witnessed one time in the history of this game in Nevada. This was a 35¢ High-Low, which was a very popular wager until the 1960s, and the player won $1,296.00.

It's not necessary to catch all of the spots on some tickets in order to win large amounts. Many wins of $10,000 and more are paid for catches of less than all the spots being played. The over-all odds of each catch on all tickets are about the same as the probability of each catch, for a minimum wager, so the amount of spots to play depends on the amount of win desired, the degree of chance a player wishes to take and the amount of his wager.

Wagering Methods

Many tickets are played for amounts up to about $50 and some are played for a few hundred dollars, but the minimum wager is still very popular. Occasionally a player will play many tickets on one drawing, sometimes up to two or three hundred, while the usual amount is from two to about six. When a great many tickets are played they are usually played for the minimum wager — seldom for more than twice the minimum wager price.

Most of the tickets played contain a single wager; that is, a straight ticket with one wager on one amount of spots, such as that shown in figure 4. These are the type of ticket wagers that are shown in all rate schedules; they are often referred to as "straight tickets," as opposed to "way tickets." These tickets form the basis of all ticket wagers and pay rates.

The Chinese, when speaking of the ways on the old 8 way ticket shown on page 132, referred to them as: One way high-low, six way 9, and one way straight. (The only ticket that was considered straight at that time was the 10 spot.)

Way tickets are increasing in popularity and there are so many different methods in which they may be marked

185

and wagered on that no particular one seems outstanding. Perhaps the more common types are groups of 5 spots played as 10 spot ways, groups of 4 spots played as 8 spot ways and groups of 3 spots played as 9 spot ways and also as 6 spot ways. Tickets marked with groups of 2 spots (deuces) are also popular and these are often played for the way combinations of 2s, 4s, 6s, 8s, and 10s. Way tickets with groups of unequal sizes are played also but are somewhat less popular.

One spot and 2 spot tickets are seldom played for a wager that is sufficient to win $25,000. Such wagers are occasionally made on 3 spot and 4 spot tickets and are frequently made on tickets with 5 or more spots. Wagers are also often made in amounts sufficient to win the limit by catching less than all the spots being played. According to the 1978 special $1.00 rate, a $2 wager on the 14 spot ticket will win the limit by catching 12 spots, while a $25.00 bet will win the limit by catching only 10 spots. The 8 spot ticket is frequently played for $14.00, which is sufficient to win the limit with a catch of 7 spots, and is occasionally played for more, sometimes up to $30.00.

A wager on any straight ticket of an amount that can win more than the payout limit, of course, increases the expected house percentage; it decreases the player's expected return in the same proportion. This is created by a decrease in the percentage amounts which are paid out for catches that win an amount greater than the payout limit. (A win of more than the payout limit is reduced to this limit for the payoff.) This change in the expected percentages varies with each ticket and with each amount wagered. As more spots are played the effect of this change lessens because the percentages paid out for these greater catches are smaller. (See percentages in figure 49.) A wager of $25 on a 14 spot ticket increases the expected house percentage over that of a 70¢ wager, but by such a small amount that it's negligible, while the same wager on an 8 spot ticket increases the house edge to more than fifty percent. This great difference is caused by two large percentage payouts being affected; the 8 spot and 7 spot catches. The results of this effect is shown below for a comparison to that of the percentages in figure 49. All percentages in figure 49 are based on the minimum wager pay rate, and are the same for any wager up to an amount that can win no more than the payout limit.

$30.00 8 Spot Ticket		
Catch	Win	% Payout
5	$ 210.00	12.8%
6	2,400.00	18.9%
7	25,000.00	13.3%
8	25,000.00	.36
Total Payout		45.4%

The percentages change.

These results illustrate the effect of this large wager and how it changes the percentages on the money paid out for the two greater catches. If proportional wagers were made on tickets with fewer than 8 spots this effect would be even greater, but such tickets are seldom ever played.

Wagers in large amounts like this can always be apportioned to increase the player's expected win by applying a part of the bet to a lesser amount of spots than the total marked on the ticket. A way ticket serves this purpose. An example of the difference in payoffs is shown below for a $28 wager on a ticket marked with 8 spots. (Special $1.00 rates of 1978.)

	$28.00 8 spot	$28.00 8 Way 7 Spot	$28.00 28 Way 6 Spot
Catch	Win	Win	Win
4	—0—	—0—	18.00
5	196.00	350.00	345.00
6	2,240.00	3,570.00	3.745.00
7	25,000.00	25,000.00	19,600.00
8	25,000.00	25,000.00	25,000.00

Wins for the same 8 spots played differently.

Of these first two wagers the 8 way 7 spot would win the most money and the 28 way 6 spot ticket would be expected to win even more. These same 8 spots could be

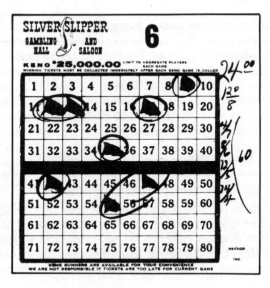

Figures 67 & 68. These two multiple way tickets are the type that often win a "bundle."

played in many other ways which would increase the wins for the smaller catches and also increase the overall expected win.

The smaller catches occur more frequently and, for this reason, tickets similar to those shown in figures 67 and 68 are occasionally played. Neither of these tickets would win the limit with a catch of 7 spots, but either would produce a win with a catch of 2 or more spots; a catch of 5 spots could produce quite a large win. Tickets like these are often played with the larger portion of the wager applied to the amount of spots that the player expects or hopes to catch. There are also many other methods in which these same spots could be grouped and played.

A wager on the 9 spot ticket of an amount that will win the limit with a catch of 8 spots effects the odds very little, and as more spots are played such wagers effect the odds even less because the greater catches pay a lesser percentage of the amount wagered.

The only practical effect that a large wager can have on the odds of a way ticket is just to the extent of the

Figure 69. Another multiple way ticket that wins often.

189

amount wagered on each way and is about the same as that of a straight ticket wager. Otherwise, the total amount wagered on any way ticket, regardless of how much, has no practical effect on the odds.

A very large and unlikely catch would be required to win the limit on the ticket in figure 69 — a win of a few thousand dollars is much more probable. The shorter odds are played in the 3 spots, the wager on the 6s provide longer odds, and the 9s and 15 spot wagers provide long and extremely long odds. This ticket is often played for only the 9 spot ways, and sometimes only the 6s are played. The 12 spot ways are also sometimes played.

Figure 70. A multiple combination way ticket.

The 10 spot wagers on the above ticket are the same as those in figure 18. The kings are added to create more ways, of a lesser amount of spots, and to increase the potential win. Unlike the tickets shown in figures 67 and 68, a catch of less than 5 spots within any combination on this ticket does not produce a win. And a catch of 5 spots which include both kings will not produce a win on the 8 spot and 9 spot wagers. But these wagers do greatly increase the win for most 5 spot catches and all catches of 6 spots and more.

190

Way tickets are more likely to win large amounts, as well as any amount, than straight tickets because they provide more ways of producing wins. The arrangements

Figure 71. Many large wins are paid out on this type of way ticket.

1	2	3	4	5	6	7	8	9	10
11	12	13	14	15	16	17	18	19	20
21	22	23	24	25	26	27	28	29	30
31	32	33	34	35	36	37	38	39	40
41	42	43	44	45	46	47	48	49	50
51	52	53	54	55	56	57	58	59	60
61	62	63	64	65	66	67	68	69	70
71	72	73	74	75	76	77	78	79	80

Figures 72 & 73. Tickets like these are frequently played and also often win large amounts.

played on way tickets are often selected on the same basis as that of straight tickets: that is, the amount of win desired is compared to the degree of chance taken along with the amount of the wager.

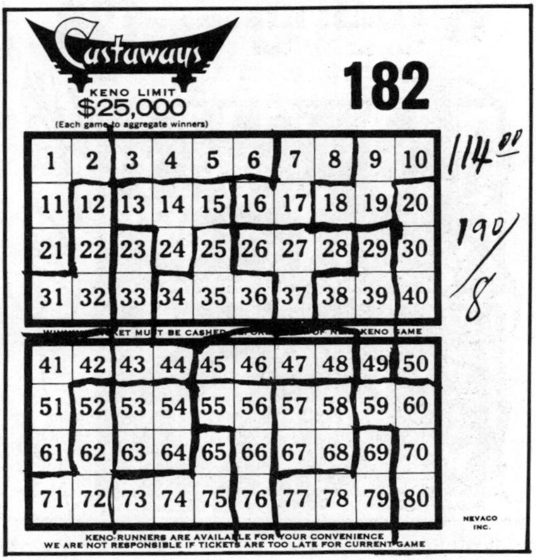

Figure 73.

Way tickets with groups of 4 spots are very popular, and the 4s are often played as such with up to about six groups. With as many groups as on the above tickets, the 4s are seldom played and the 12 spot ways are never played. The 190 way 8 spot ticket is very popular and it is usually marked as shown in figure 72, but it is sometimes marked into square or other shaped groups and is occasionally marked with odd-shaped groups as shown in figure 73.

These tickets carry the same long odds as a single 8 spot wager and, because they provide many ways of producing wins, various size wins, including the limit, occur very frequently.

There are several popular methods in which all eighty of the ticket numbers are played, other than those previously shown. Some of these methods are illustrated in figures 74 through 80.

192

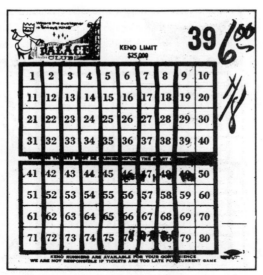

Figures 74 through 80. These way tickets make use of all 80 numbers and some of them are played frequently.

Figure 75

Some of these tickets make up many ways while others make use of larger groups, creating a lesser amount of ways. The likeliness of a win on each is proportional to

193

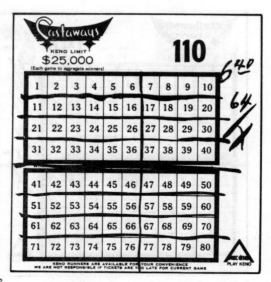

Figure 76

Figure 77

the amount of ways played and the amount of spots in each way. There are also many other methods in which all of the numbers may be grouped and played.

194

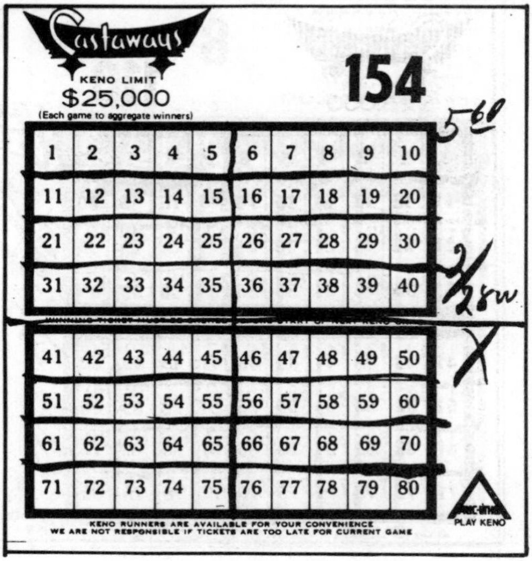

Figure 78

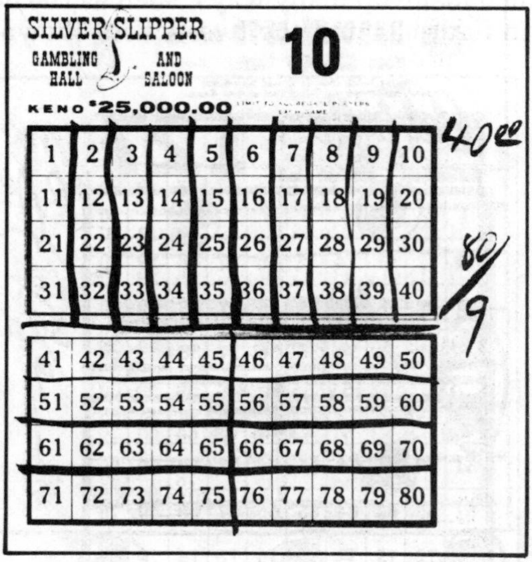

Figure 79

Figure 80

Some way tickets are played that are marked with few spots which make up many ways, such as the deuce-way 10 spot in figure 34 and the two tickets shown below.

Figure 81. A way ticket producing many ways with few spots. A winning catch on this ticket can produce wins on many of the ways.

196

Figure 82. An unusual 7 way 8 spot ticket.

Because of the many combinations that are made up from a few spots on these tickets, a medium size catch may produce a win on several or many of the ways. Tickets like these may produce very large wins with a catch of just a few spots.

Sometimes only the short odds are played on tickets that are marked with many spots. Tickets marked into groups of 4s, such as in figure 72, are occasionally played as a 20 way 4 spot only. Tickets like that in figure 34 are sometimes played for only the 2 spot wagers. While these tickets cannot win a large sum, a small win is quite likely.

Once a ticket marked with 8 spots was grouped and played as two 4s for a 25¢ wager on each. All 8 spots were caught and the ticket won $59.00. Of course, a large enough wager on either of the 4s, or this amount wagered on both would have won the limit, which was $25,000, but a wager of only $1.10 on the 8 spot would also have won the limit. Similar incidents have occurred with 6 spots played as two 3s.

197

Figure 83. An unusual 8 way 9 spot.

Many tickets, similar to the one above, are often played for just a portion of the existing ways. Each of the 2 groups of 4 spots on this ticket are used with each 5 spot group to make up the 9 spot ways, but the 4s are not used together as the 8 spot is not being played. A catch of all 8 spots within the 4 spot groups and none in the 5 spot groups would win only pittance on the old pay-4 rate and nothing on the pay-5 rates, while an additional $1.00 or $1.40 wager on the 8 spot would win $25,000. A similar siutation also exists with the 10 spot ways.

The 6 spot ticket is very popular and these spots are often grouped into 2s and played as three 2s or as three 4s or both, in addition to the 6 spot wager. The spots are also sometimes grouped as shown in figure 84, creating 3 spot wagers as well as 2s and 4s. By grouping only one deuce the ticket is occasionally played as one 6 spot and one 2 spot.

It has been the custom to include in the rate pamphlets a few suggested way tickets. These are always of the more common types and are listed to introduce different types of ticket wagers, thereby promoting a further interest in the game. The pamphlets do not fully explain these

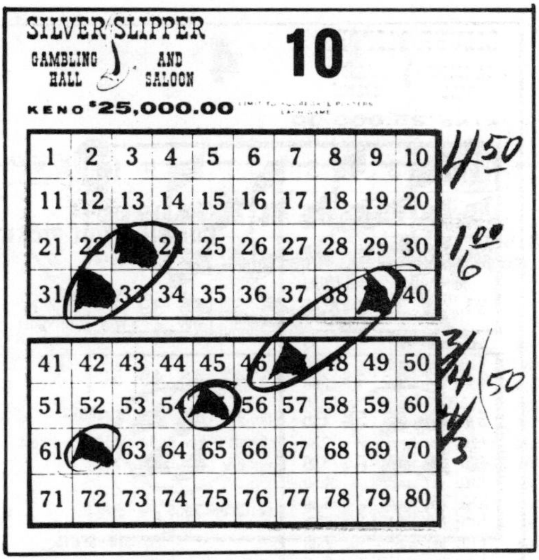

Figure 84. A multiple way ticket that wins often.

wagers but the dealers (writers) will gladly explain any ticket that a player inquires about. Shown in figure 85 are some of these suggestions that are commonly listed.

Some of these tickets have previously been illustrated and discussed, such as the "Japanese King — 12 way" shown in figure 24 on page 95. This illustration shows the ticket played as an 11 way 10 spot only, however, the field of 9 spots is usually also played as a 9 spot wager, as it is suggested here. The term "king ticket" refers to any way ticket which contains any amount of kings. Some of these tickets have been known by various names in different clubs, however they are not generally known throughout the industry anymore by any particular name.

Shown in figure 86 is the "18 spot king ticket" referred to in the suggested way tickets. This ticket is seldom played anymore but was very popular for many years. The two 9 spot wagers are made up of the spots within each group (each group contains 9 spots). The 10 spot ways are made up from the arrangement of all the kings within one group plus one king from the other group. Or this same arrangement may be viewed as using each

199

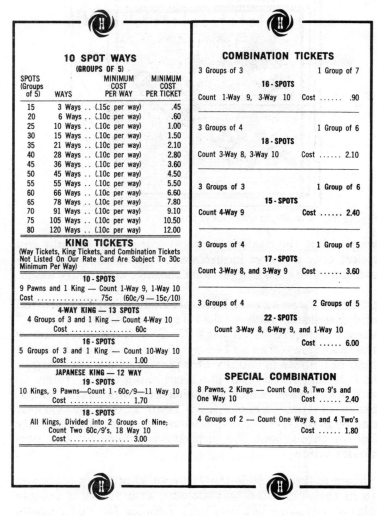

10 SPOT WAYS
(GROUPS OF 5)

SPOTS (Groups of 5)	WAYS		MINIMUM COST PER WAY	MINIMUM COST PER TICKET
15	3 Ways	.. (.15c per way)		.45
20	6 Ways	.. (.10c per way)		.60
25	10 Ways	.. (.10c per way)		1.00
30	15 Ways	.. (.10c per way)		1.50
35	21 Ways	.. (.10c per way)		2.10
40	28 Ways	.. (.10c per way)		2.80
45	36 Ways	.. (.10c per way)		3.60
50	45 Ways	.. (.10c per way)		4.50
55	55 Ways	.. (.10c per way)		5.50
60	66 Ways	.. (.10c per way)		6.60
65	78 Ways	.. (.10c per way)		7.80
70	91 Ways	.. (.10c per way)		9.10
75	105 Ways	.. (.10c per way)		10.50
80	120 Ways	.. (.10c per way)		12.00

KING TICKETS
(Way Tickets, King Tickets, and Combination Tickets Not Listed On Our Rate Card Are Subject To 30c Minimum Per Way)

10 - SPOTS
9 Pawns and 1 King — Count 1-Way 9, 1-Way 10
Cost .... 75c   (60c/9 — 15c/10)

4-WAY KING — 13 SPOTS
4 Groups of 3 and 1 King — Count 4-Way 10
Cost 60c

16 - SPOTS
5 Groups of 3 and 1 King — Count 10-Way 10
Cost 1.00

JAPANESE KING — 12 WAY
19 - SPOTS
10 Kings, 9 Pawns—Count 1 - 60c/9—11 Way 10
Cost 1.70

18 - SPOTS
All Kings, Divided into 2 Groups of Nine;
Count Two 60c/9's, 18 Way 10
Cost 3.00

COMBINATION TICKETS

3 Groups of 3   1 Group of 7
16 - SPOTS
Count 1-Way 9, 3-Way 10   Cost ...... .90

3 Groups of 4   1 Group of 6
18 - SPOTS
Count 3-Way 8, 3-Way 10   Cost 2.10

3 Groups of 3   1 Group of 6
15 - SPOTS
Count 4-Way 9   Cost 2.40

3 Groups of 4   1 Group of 5
17 - SPOTS
Count 3-Way 8, and 3-Way 9   Cost 3.60

3 Groups of 4   2 Groups of 5
22 - SPOTS
Count 3-Way 8, 6-Way 9, and 1-Way 10
Cost 6.00

SPECIAL COMBINATION
8 Pawns, 2 Kings — Count One 8, Two 9's and One Way 10   Cost 2.40

4 Groups of 2 — Count One Way 8, and 4 Two's
Cost 1.80

Figure 85. Suggested ticket wagers from Harolds Club.

Figure 86

Figures 86 & 87. These two ancient way tickets were devised by the Chinese many years ago.

king, one at a time, with the 9 spots in the other group, which makes 9 ways from each side and a total of 18 ways.

201

It is customary to king all the spots on a ticket like this, however, except for this custom, it would not really be necessary as there is no reason to differentiate between the spots within each group. Figure 87 illustrates the method used to mark the spots on this ticket when the groups are so arranged as to be inconvenient to separate them with a line.

This ticket is usually played only as these two are conditioned, however, like the ticket shown in figure 54, it could be played for thousands of different ways.

Figure 88. Another old Chinese way ticket, known as "Poor Man King."

The 4 way 10 spot in figure 88 was very popular from before the turn of the century until during the 1960s. It's seldom seen anymore. Figure 89 shows another moderately priced ticket that was often played. The ticket shown in figure 90 is marked the same as the old 8 way, which is shown in figure 41. Very few clubs write the High-Low ticket anymore so the wager as conditioned here is sometimes played.

Figure 89. Another way ticket that originated with the Chinese.

Figure 90. A way ticket grouped like the old 8 way.

Shown in figure 91 are suggested wagers that were published by some of the Chinese-American games during the 1920s. These suggested tickets may seem even more confusing than those in figure 85 because these descriptions are more condensed. Also the "King Tickets" and "Full Ticket King" wagers referred to do not contain any kings, as kings are known today. However, these wagers were clearly understood by the regular players, which were then mostly Chinese. The ways on the first suggestion, "Way Ticket, 5¢ Rate," are 10 spot ways and are made up of groups containing 5 spots in each, like the tickets in figures 17, 20 and 77. The suggestion states the number of spots involved but fails to mention that they are divided into groups of 5 spots in each. The next suggestion, "King Tickets, 5¢ Way," are 10 spot way tickets which are marked with groups containing 4 spots in each and groups containing

WAY TICKET, 5-CENT RATE		
15 spots	3 ways cost	$ .15
20 spots	6 ways cost	.30
25 spots	10 ways cost	.50
30 spots	15 ways cost	.75
35 spots	21 ways cost	1.05
40 spots	28 ways cost	1.40
45 spots	36 ways cost	1.80
50 spots	45 ways cost	2.25
55 spots	55 ways cost	2.75
60 spots	66 ways cost	3.30
65 spots	78 ways cost	3.90
70 spots	91 ways cost	4.55
75 spots	105 ways cost	5.25
80 spots	120 ways cost	6.00

KING TICKETS, 5-CENT WAY		
14 spots	5 ways cost	$ .25
18 spots	12 ways cost	.60
22 spots	22 ways cost	1.10
26 spots	35 ways cost	1.75
30 spots	51 ways cost	2.55

POOR MAN KING, 5-CENT WAY		
16 spots	4 ways cost	$ .20
19 spots	8 ways cost	.40
22 spots	15 ways cost	.75

JAPANESE KING TICKET		
19 spots	10 King 9 Men cost	$ .90

HIGH-LOW WAY TICKET, 35-CENT WAY		
16 spots	4 ways cost	$ 1.40
20 spots	10 ways cost	3.50
24 spots	20 ways cost	7.00
28 spots	35 ways cost	12.25
32 spots	56 ways cost	19.60

9 SPOT WAY TICKET, 35-CENT WAY		
13 spots	3 ways cost	$ 1.05
17 spots	6 ways cost	2.10
21 spots	10 ways cost	3.50

$2.80 COMBINATION TICKET
35-CENT EACH WAY

22 Spots Mark 2 Sets 5, 3 Sets 4
Count 6-9 Spots. 1 High-Low
1 Way Straight

$1.40 COMBINATION TICKET
35-CENT EACH WAY

17 Spots
Mark 1 Set 5, 3 Sets 4
Counts 3-9 Spots. 1 High-Low

FULL TICKET KING, 5-CENT WAY		
8 and 2	36 ways	$ 1.80
7 and 3	24 ways	1.20
6 and 4	18 ways	.90
5 and 5	15 ways	.75

Figure 91. Suggested ticket wagers that were printed on some of the Chinese rate schedules.

2 spots (deuces) in each. Each of the tickets listed contain three deuces, but each is marked with a different amount of 4 spot groups. Two 4 spot groups make 5 ways, three 4 spot groups make 12 ways, four 4 spot groups make 22 ways, five 4 spot groups make 35 ways, and six 4 spot groups make up 51 ways. These tickets are still played but only on rare occasions.

The tickets known as "Poor Man King" are also 10 spot way tickets. Each of these tickets is marked with one field of 6 spots and with one king. Then different amounts of 3 spot groups are used to make up different amounts of ways. The 4 way ticket is marked with three 3 spot groups, four 3 spot groups make up 8 ways, and the 15 way ticket is marked with five groups of 3 spots.

The spots on the "High-Low Way Tickets" are divided into groups of 4 spots in each.

These "9 Spot Way Tickets" are marked with groups containing 4 spots, plus one king.

The "Japanese King Ticket" is the same as that suggested in figure 85.

The "$2.80 Combination Ticket" is the same as the 8 way shown in figure 41.

The "$1.40 Combination Ticket" is the old 4 way described on page 133.

The "Full Ticket King" is seldom played anymore but was quite popular in the early days. These are 10 spot way tickets and the one which makes up 36 ways is marked with one group of 8 spots and 36 deuces, making use of all eighty numbers. These ways are made up by couting the 8 spot group with each of the deuces. The arrangement of 5 deuces is not used. The 24 way ticket is marked with one group of 7 spots and 24 groups of 3 spots. The 18 way ticket is marked with one group of 6 spots and 18 groups of 4 spots. And the 15 way ticket is marked with 16 groups of 5 numbers in each, again using all eighty numbers. Then spots are marked on the numbers in just one of these groups to indicate that this group is used with each of the others to make up the 15 ways. A common method of marking this ticket is like that in figure 77.

The number of ways in which a Keno wager can be made would seemingly run into infinity. It has been said that there has not yet been enough paper manufactured to record all of these possible ways. This, of course, is not correct but was said to emphasize the greatness of number.

Of all these different tickets and methods of wagering it can be seen that some, like the example on page 187, increase the expected percentage for the house and may be termed a "poor ticket" for the player. There is no method of marking a ticket that will increase the mathematical percentage for the player over that of a straight ticket at a minimum wager.

So the "best ticket" to play is still a matter of choice and is whichever ticket that wins best for the player.

Winnings Reported

On April 1, 1968 a requirement became effective whereby certain Keno winnings were reported, quarterly, by the casinos to the Internal Revenue Service. These reports were made on Form 1099, U. S. Information Returns, and each listed the winner's name, address and the amount of the payoff. All payoffs of $10,000 or more were subject to this reporting requirement, and payoffs of lesser amounts were reported on a sliding scale related to the amount wagered:

The "amount wagered" applied only to the cost of the winning ticket and did not include the cost of any other tickets which may have also been played. For example: If a player played two 60¢ tickets and one of them won $1,250.00 this win was reported. However, if these two wagers were combined on one ticket the ticket cost would be $1.20 and this win would have been without the reporting category. On way tickets, the amount wagered on each way was not considered; *it was the cost of the ticket that determined the category.*

In the case of add-tickets, the total amount wagered determined the category because this total wager was recorded on one ticket.

SCALE OF REPORTABLE KENO PAYOFFS		
Total Price of Ticket		Payoffs Reportable
from	through	
$ 0	$ .59	$ 600.00 or more
.60	.89	1,200.00 or more
.90	1.19	1,800.00 or more
1.20	1.79	2,400.00 or more
1.80	2.39	3,000.00 or more
2.40	2.99	3,600.00 or more
3.00	3.59	4,200.00 or more
3.60	9.99	6,000.00 or more
10.00	and over	10,000.00 or more

Payoffs reported on IRS form 1099.

Should a winning ticket which fell within the reporting category be played by a number of partners, the report was made on one form in the name of the person receiving payment. (It was suggested by the Internal Revenue Service that the person receiving the payment would report his share of the winnings and the names and addresses of the other winners on his individual income tax return.)

A similar requirement was in effect for a short time during the 1950s. Winners at that time were not required to furnish identification and so many fictitious names were reported (*Joe Blow* was popular) that the requirement was soon withdrawn. With this new rule a winner was required to furnish reasonable identification and the giving of a fake or fictitious name, address and social security number subjected the winner to criminal penalties.

In March 1977 a new Internal Revenue Service regulation became effective. This one required the casinos to report to the IRS *a payout of $1,000 or more without considering the cost of the wager*. This meant that if a player paid $1,000 for a ticket and won back just the amount of the wager (*this is possible*) a report would be sent to IRS that would look as though a win had been paid.

Within a few weeks this rule was amended to require the casinos to report a *net win payout of $1,500 or more after deducting the cost of the ticket*. These reports are made on a new form known as "*W-2G.*" The casinos are not required at this time to withhold any tax from these wins, but these forms have a space for "Federal Income Tax Withheld" so the next rule change may make use of this space.

The filing of these information returns merely gives notice of such wins, and the amount of income tax due from winnings is determined from the net gain, as in other forms of income. All gambling wins must be included in gross income, however, sec. 1.165-10 of the Income Tax Regulations provides for the deducting of gambling losses:

> "*WAGERING LOSSES. — Losses sustained during the taxable year on wagering transactions shall be allowed as a deduction but only to the extent of the gains during the taxable year from such transactions. In the case of a husband and wife making a joint return for the taxable year, the combined losses of the spouses from wagering transactions shall be allowed to the extent of the combined gains of the spouses from wagering transactions.*"

The Internal Revenue Service states that it is not possible to specify the exact records that every taxpayer should maintain to substantiate gambling wins and losses. However, they suggest that, as a minimum, taxpayers should maintain a day-by-day account of wins and losses which include:

(1) Date of gambling transaction.

(2) Name of person (if individual), casino, bookie, race track, etc., with whom wager was placed.

(3) Location — city and state.

(4) Type of game or games played.

(5) The amount of the win and the loss, or a net daily figure.

This record may be in the form of a diary made at or near the time of the wins and losses. The taxpayer will be required on request of IRS to corroborate entries by furnishing other collateral evidence, such as savings account pass books, cancelled checks cashed on day of loss, proof of presence at casino or place of gambling at time of loss, or statements of third parties (casino employees or other witnesses). So it is important to keep a complete record of gambling wins and losses, like other types of income and expenses, in order to determine the correct income tax liability.

Players often tip the Keno writers when receiving a large win and these gratuities are also income which must be accounted for. All of this money is usually declared as tip income and reported to Internal Revenue Service on form 4070. Because of the manner in which some of this money is received it may not all be tip income. Some of it may be considered as gambling winnings. This condition is created when a player gives a portion of the bet to the writer while the ticket is being written. Players do this sometimes by telling the writer that if the ticket hits a big win it will be split in some certain way with the writers. In effect, the player is giving the writers a percentage of the cost of the ticket and betting it for him. If the ticket wins and the writers share in this windfall this amount would be a gambling win.

Whether the money is a tip or a gambling win, it is still income which must be accounted for in order to determine the income tax liability. Its source should also be considered because this might make a substantial difference in the amount of tax to be paid. There are usually no special deductions allowed from tip income and the whole amount is taxable, in the same manner as wages. So for the average taxpayer tips just increase the gross income. Gambling wins are different, however, because only the net amount (wins less losses) is taxable. Because all gambling losses throughout the year are deductable, up to the amount of the wins, any gambling losses a writer might have would reduce his tax liability on the portion of money that is gambling winnings.

In about 1972, on a game in Reno, a customer tipped the writers by playing a one dollar ticket for them. After his own tickets were written he gave a dollar to the writer as he was walking away and said, "Here, mark a ticket for the boys." This writer marked a ticket and it won $3,440. (It was the first such winning ticket he had ever marked since he started working on the games in 1938.) This whole amount was a gambling win.

The story goes a step further and is most unusual. The win fell within the category of those reported to Internal Revenue Service, and the writer who had written the ticket didn't want his name to be reported as the winner because he thought that he would be "stuck" for paying all the tax, even though the whole amount of the win was to be divided among all the writers. This writer was acquainted with the customer who had paid for the ticket, so he asked the customer to use his name as the winner on the report, for which he would be paid half the win. The customer accepted this and put the $1,720.00 in his pocket. An equal sum was shared equally among all the writers.

This transaction creates a very unusual situation. Except for $1, the full amount of the win was gambling winnings won by the writers working on the game. While the full amount ($3,440.00) belonged to the writers, they could do with it whatever they pleased — so they chose to give half of it to another party. But the writers are still liable for the income tax on the whole amount. (That is, if there were no gambling losses to offset it.) The customer is liable for another tax on the amount he received, and for him this is not a gambling win. It would be a fee for the use of his name on the report form.

More than $500 million is paid out annually in Keno winnings; this, of course, represents a great number of winning pays, considering that more than fifty percent of it is in amounts of less than $20 and about five percent in amounts of less than $1.00. Less than three percent of the total amount paid out falls within the reporting category. Different brackets of winning amounts are listed below, showing the approximate percentage of the total amount paid out that is represented by each.

Amount of Win			% of Total
less than	$	5.00	15.1 %
$ 5.00	to	9.95	17.8
10.00	to	19.95	20.7
20.00	to	49.95	27.1
50.00	to	499.95	12.9
500.00	and over		6.4

These figures are the results of the rate schedules and the trend in the way most tickets are played. A change in this trend of playing tickets (average cost of ticket and how the wagers are applied) will cause these percentage figures to change somewhat from time to time.

Gamble To Win

It seems that a fear of losing can actually prevent a player from winning. Just why this happens is not known, but it is realized by many that when a player is playing in a relaxed atmosphere, free of worry and within his financial bounds, he is more likely to win.

This theory about fear was demonstrated one evening by a young man who had won $10 on his ticket. The ticket was presented to a writer; the writer, not knowing there was a win on it, wrote the ticket before the man timidly stated, in a doubtful manner, that the ticket had won. The writer then checked the ticket and, after paying the win, asked if he wished to replay it. The player first started to pay for the new ticket, but after hesitating for

211

a moment decided to not replay it. His fear of losing on the next game was quite obvious even though the cost of the ticket was only $1.10. This was an 8 spot ticket, and 7 of these numbers were drawn on the next game, which would have produced a $2,200.00 win.

In the same club and within a few days after this incident a middle-aged Oriental man demonstrated a theory on the lack of fear. He was playing a 50¢ 6 spot ticket and caught 5 spots, winning $55. He presented the ticket to a writer, stating firmly that it was a winner and that he would replay it for a $5 wager. All 6 numbers were drawn on the next game and he won $6,200.00.

It's incidents like these that cause the belief that fear of losing and other annoying disturbances create a situation which lessens the chances of winning. So it has been said that, when gambling, know the game you are playing — and gamble to win.

Good Luck!

GLOSSARY

ACTION: The volume of betting.

ADD-TICKET: A ticket used to register the bet of other tickets.

AGENT: A person outside the game who transacts ticket wagers.

BANK: The game's operating funds. Money.

BASKET: The receptical from which the balls are drawn.

BET: The amount of money played on a ticket. A wager.

BODY: The numbered area of a ticket.

BOOK: The inside tickets after they are bound. Also the perforated (dated) numbered paper that is bound (usually with a clamp) in preparation for punching the draws.

CAGE: The receptical from which the balls are drawn.

CALL: To announce the numbers of the balls as they are drawn.

CAP: A closer.

CARRYOVER: A ticket played for two or more games and paid for in advance.

CATCH: The amount of winning numbers that appear within the marked numbers of a ticket.

CHASE: To change the numbers played each game.

CHECK—TICKET: A ticket which wins an amount that is paid according to the inside ticket.

CHIP or CHECK: A token used instead of money for placing bets.

CIRCLE: A line drawn around a group of spots.

CLOSE: The time, during the drawing of each game, when no ticket wagers are taken.

CLOSER: A blank ticket on which is stamped a serial number at the close of each game. The back side of a draw is often used.

COMBINATION TICKET: A ticket with a combination of wagers on varying amounts of spots.

COME UP: The drawing of a keno ball. The number came up.

COMING OUT: The beginning of the drawing of a game.

CONDITION: The manner in which a ticket wager is made. A ticket is conditioned to indicate how the wager is applied.

COPY: To write a player's ticket. The duplicate of the player's ticket.

CUT: A line drawn through a ticket separating groups of marked spots.

DEALER: One who works on the game. A writer.

DESK: The area in which the wagers of record are kept.

DEUCE: A group containing two spots.

DOUBLE KENO: Two keno games at one counter.

DRAW: A blank ticket showing the winning numbers that were drawn by punching a hole through those numbers. A specific race, game or drawing.

DRILL: A device used to make holes in the draws. Also to punch, or drill, the book.

DUPLICATE: The player's ticket copy.

ERROR: A mistake in the marking of a ticket wager.

EXACTA PARLAY: A special bet on Club Cal-Neva's Double Action Keno game.

FACE VALUE: The amount that a ticket has won.

FAT SPOT: A large marked spot, overlapping into another number.

FIELD: An uncircled group of spots.

FIX: To fix a fictitious winning ticket.

FLASHBOARD: A numbered board showing the results of each drawing by lighting the winning numbers.

GAME: The keno game in general. A specific game or drawing.

GOOSE: The receptacle from which the balls are drawn.

GROUP: Any amount of spots separated from others on a ticket.

HEAD-TICKET: A winning ticket that is paid from the desk bank rather than from a writer's bank. (This applies only to the very few games that operate with individual banks for each writer.)

HIT: A winning catch. The ticket hit for a big win. The game was hit for the limit.

HORSE: A ticket number.

HOUSE: A gaming establishment.

INSIDE TICKET: The original ticket. The wager of record.

KING: A group containing one spot.

KING TICKET: A ticket which contains any amount of kings.

LIMIT: A set amount limiting the game's liabilities for losses.

LINE: A line drawn through a ticket separating marked spots or played numbers.

LIVE TICKET: Either copy of a played ticket before the results of the drawing are known or, in the case of a win, before the win is paid.

MARGIN: That portion of a ticket outside the numbered area.

MARK: To make spots on a ticket. To mark a ticket for play.

MISCONDITIONED: A ticket conditioned incorrectly.

MISMARK: To spot the player's copy different from the original ticket.

MISSPOT: A spot that is not marked on a specific number and does not indicate which number is to be played.

MULTIPLE TICKET: A ticket containing two or more individual wagers, each independent of the other.

NEW BOOK: To make another book of draws after a wrong-hole was punched in the first book. The first book was "blown."

NEW TICKET: A ticket played for the first time.

ODDS: A ratio expressing the likeliness of the occurrence of an event. A ratio of the win to the wager.

OPEN: The time between drawings during which tickets are written.

OPENER: A paper, usually a blank ticket, on which is stamped a serial number prior to writing tickets for each drawing. Each writer makes an opener and the serial number of all tickets written on a drawing will follow the number on these openers. On some games a closing number, after all tickets are written, is also stamped on the opener.

ORIGINAL TICKET: The ticket submitted for play by the player.

OUTSTATION: An annex where tickets are written.

OUTSIDE TICKET: The duplicate copy of a player's wager.

PAPER: Unmarked blank tickets.
    INSIDE PAPER: Numbered blank tickets used by the writers.
    OUTSIDE PAPER: Unnumbered blank tickets used by the players.
    LIVE PAPER: Numbered blank tickets of the game being written.
    OLD PAPER: Numbered blank tickets of the game number that was just previously written.
    NEW PAPER: Numbered blank tickets of the game number to be written next.

PARLAY: To bet the winnings from one game on another game.

PATTERN: The arrangement of the winning numbers.

PAWN: A spot within a field.

PERCENTAGE (PC): The mathematical percentage in favor of the house. The house edge.

PERFORATE: To date the draws by perforating.

PIT TICKET: A ticket played by one who is also participating in a table game.

PLAY: To make a bet. To wager.

POST TIME: When the balls are replaced in the receptacle and a game is almost ready to be drawn.

PUNCH: Device used to make holes in the draws. To make draws by drilling or punching.

RACE: A drawing. A specific game.

RACK: A receptacle for holding the drawn balls.

RATE (PAY RATE): The amounts won for the different winning catches for a given ticket price.

REPLAYED TICKET: A played ticket that was recently previously played.

ROAD MAP: A ticket marked with lines separating odd-shaped groups. (Like than shown in figure 73.)

RUN-DOWN: A blank ticket on which is noted the numerical sequence of the drawn winning numbers.

RUNNER: One who carries tickets, wagers and wins between players and the game.

SLEEPER: A winning ticket that is not cashed in.

SPECIAL: A rate of winning pays that is different from the usual.

SPOT: A mark indicating a played number. To mark a spot.

STRAIGHT TICKET: A single wager on one amount of spots.

TICKET: Marked paper. The paper on which a keno wager is made.

WAGER: To play a ticket. A bet.

WAIT: To continue playing the same numbers each game.

WAY TICKET: A ticket with the spots so grouped as to provide two or more arrangements that are wagered on.

WIN: A winning pay of any amount, even if it's less than the wager.

217

WINNING NUMBERS: The twenty numbers that are drawn each game.

WRITE: To make a duplicate of a player's ticket. The wagers of record.

WRITER: One who works on the game and writes tickets.

ABOUT THE AUTHOR

Wayne McClure knows Keno as a player and as one who has worked behind the Keno counter. He dealt the game for many years in Reno and South Lake Tahoe. As a player he has the distinction of hitting **a limit $25,000 ticket on Dec. 7, 1976** at Harvey's Wagon Wheel, South Lake Tahoe. This fantastic event happened 35 years to the day after another important event. (Wayne was aboard a destroyer in Pearl Harbor, Dec. 7, 1941.)

He received his early gambling experience as a teenager in the back rooms of gambling halls in his home town in Texas. He travelled with a carnival and at 16 ran a grift midway game. An 8-year Navy stint continued his education in gambling.

Although having researched Keno for over 15 years, Wayne feels his work on the game is just starting. With the release of his book, he expects and will welcome comments. Anyone wishing to make additions for inclusion in the next edition may write **Wayne McClure,** in care of the publisher.